HOW
TO
PUT
YOURSELF
ACROSS

HOW TO
PUT YOURSELF
ACROSS

Elmer Wheeler

PRENTICE-HALL, INC., Englewood Cliffs, N. J.

WORLD-WIDE AUTHOR

ELMER WHEELER's books have been translated into six languages and published in 20 foreign editions. In the United States, some 70 printings testify to the popularity of this world-wide author and expert on selling techniques.

How to Make Your Daydreams Come True (3 printings)

How to Make Your Sales Sizzle in 17 Days (2 printings)

How to Sell Yourself To Others (17 printings)

Tested Sentences That Sell (19 printings)

Sizzlemanship: New Tested Sentences (10 printings)

Tested Public Speaking (13 printings)

Tested Retail Selling (6 printings)

Selling Dangerously (4 printings)

Tested Selling Tips From Around the World
(recently published)

Dedication

To Archie Hunter,
who never really retired
and so is still going places.

We are a part of everything we hear,
of everybody we meet.

CONTENTS

7

HOW
TO
PUT
YOURSELF
ACROSS

1

"Cuba, Si; Yankee, No!" offers
a great lesson in how to win others
to your way of thinking
for everlasting friendship—
if used in complete reverse

> *"A friend is a present you give yourself."*
> —Robert Louis Stevenson

I moved over to Fidel Castro's table.

He had motioned me over, and I had greeted him, *"Buenas noches, Dr. Castro. Que pasa?"*

He ran his fingers through his trade-marked beard, shoved the whiskered cabbage across the banquet table toward me, and said softly, "You, *señor,* are a salesman from the U. S. Tell me, *por favor,* how can I sell myself to your people?"

I was about to respond when a photographer, overhearing Castro's plea, snapped our photos. Then as I began to gather my thoughts to tell him, a U. S. representative stood up to make a short talk at this international gathering of 2,000 members of the American Society of Travel Agents.

Somehow he was failing to sell himself to Castro with his rather weak explanation of why Havana had been bombed with leaflets, from planes supposedly from the United States. The reason for the failure of our man seemed to be in the use of too diplomatic language for Castro to accept, of words too remote for Castro to understand. Castro had an English understanding of only some 200 words. He turned his beard from me and began to glower at the diplomat floundering in wordage.

I thought it best to retreat to my table.

Presently our man sat down the distinguished president of ASTA stood up for his turn to talk. He had been down among the Cuban people that afternoon as they paraded around our hotels with signs, which read, TELL THE PEOPLE OF THE U. S. THE REAL STORY OF THE LEAFLETS. The placards signed, "Methodist Church," "Baptist Church" and so forth, were paraded in an endeavor to win over these 2,000 travel agents. He had been in the middle of the mob at times, raising his coat in one hand, gesticulating in true Cuban fashion with the other, shouting back, "We are friends, *amigos*—friends!"

The people responded to this shirt sleeved man from the United States, head of a very well-known travel firm, for they liked the way he went among them, arms in windmill fashion, always a smile on his face to assure these people that his country had nothing to do with the leaflet bombing. Castro also liked him as he spoke, for again he was talking simple language, with emotional delivery, backed up with sincere smiles.

Suddenly Castro could restrain himself no longer. He leaped to his feet and put his arms around him and shouted, "This man, I love!"

"Cuba, Si; Yankee, No!"

The student of human nature now asks:

What had the diplomat done, or failed to do, that the travel agent did to win this tyrant over?

What lessons in getting ourselves across with friends, relatives, neighbors and business associates and customers, can be learned from this critical moment in Cuban-American relations? Wherein spoken words from one annoyed a dictator, the words of another won him over in dramatic fashion, delaying the "Cuba, Si; Yankee, No!" era.

What lessons can you and I learn from this fateful banquet in Havana that preceeded an era of "Cuba, Si; Yankee, No!" sentiment in many parts of the world?

I studied the situation. Things went from bad to worse, then all the way to impossible. I have often felt that our bad relationships with Cuba began at that banquet, despite Allen's one-man attempt to prevent a situation from growing. I have since traveled clear around South America, with Panagra Airlines as my host, and have heard two sides of the story. I have visited with many South American observers. From them I have learned useful rules in putting yourself across to use in handling the recalcitrant, the stubborn, the obnoxious—rules that can also be used in your own daily life to get yourself sold to others.

There are great lessons to be learned from this night in Havana. Here began that downfall in relationships. A point where a man turned from Dr. Jekyll into Mr. Hyde because of words alone. When one man talked above the head of the person he was trying to sell, clothing his language in fine bits of diplomacy that, for the moment, was not fitting for the occasion. The other man spoke in the language of the dictator and delayed, even though momentarily, the world outbursts that we have come to know only too well from the bushy-faced one.

Perhaps Castro did not understand fully the words of the travel agent, but he felt and sensed from the tones of the speaker's voice, and his facial gestures, that here was a man who had sympathies, was sincere, and spoke from his heart and not page 13 of some diplomatic manual on procedures.

There seems a time to break away from the rule books, and this was one.

I can shout at my dog, "COME NICE DOGGIE AND GET A JUICY BONE." My tone of voice will prompt the dog to back away from me. My glare will frighten him. But should I say in sweet tones, with a smile, "Come nice doggie and get a good beating," the dog will respond to tone and gesture and come to me.

That is the first lesson to be learned: proper tone of voice and gesture in dealing with people.

For Castro had come to the banquet to make friends. He had rebuilt a revolutionary-torn airport in 45 days to welcome the 2,000 travel agents from around the world, to inspire them to return home and sell Cuba. He had planted tall palm trees from airport to hotels, lined them with placards of welcome. He had gathered $1.00 contributions from waiters all over Cuba to help pay for the banquet fiesta and the performance he planned; every popular chef in Cuba contributed food. He was prepared to sell himself to the world.

Then came the anti-Castro leaflet bombardment. He still went through with his banquet plans, then wrong words brought out the beast hidden in his whiskers. Well, you know the horrible Castro story from there on. It is part of history, not part of this book on how to put yourself across with others. But it has re-taught us the rules in winning people over.

Perhaps other situations would have arisen anyway to fire off the whiskered tyrant. You be the judge. That's not the purpose of this story. My purpose is to ascertain how we might have made the signs read, "Yankees, si' Communism, nyet!" And here are some rules that you can apply daily to win over friends, neighbors, relatives, family or to use in your business contacts:

Rule 1.   *Use Simple Words*

Too often we talk above the heads of others. We lack an understanding of the vocabulary of the ones we are trying to sell. We insult the intelligence of others with our intelligence; or we make use of words that fail to reach the hearts of others. We talk over their heads.

We are apt to flaunt our education by quoting Latin mottoes or French bon mots, or use diplomatic hogwash that fails to strike the heart, only to hit the brain a wack.

The first trick in winning over others is to use words that the other person comprehends easily and that leave no room for misunderstanding. "It saves your back," says the washing machine seller, and wins a woman over who would look in bewilderment if he had said, "This machine won't give you lumbago." Simple words strike hearts of people—complicated ones bring perplexed wrinkles on brows. So learn the art of saying something simple.

Rule 2.   *Talk Their Own Language*

With a German audience or customer, talk facts. With an Oriental, talk gently. With an Indian, step up your speed of delivery, but in a reverent Indian manner. With a U. S. audience you can jest.

Individuals, as well as countries, respond to one who speaks their own language, or failing to know the language, at least speaks words they like to hear. For example, the mid-westerner likes to hear his first name; but a New Englander likes to hear Mr. in front of his name.

Truck drivers, bookkeepers, purchasing agents, friends, neighbors—the family—like familiar sounding words, those they themselves would use. It warms them up to the other person.

Be one of them—and win them.

Rule 3.   *Smile As You Talk*

They may fail to understand what you're talking

about, but your smile disarms them. It indicates you are friendly.

In Italy, a land of great demonstrative and emotional re-actions, I have often observed two people getting into a heated curb-side argument. Small groups will gather around and take sides. On one such occasion I asked my friend, Aloschi, what the fight was about. He told me, "It is no fight, my friend. The two are merely discussing where to eat. They will have a similar lively argument in the restaurant over which sauce to have on their spaghetti. If you understand this Italian trait you will better understand the people."

I believe Aloschi's last sentence gives the trick of winning others—that is to "understand" the people you are dealing with. In that way you will fit into their likes, dislikes, moods and habits.

Soon we will see how this is done.

But for the moment, let me tell you one other experience in a land of dictators. This occurred in Santo Domingo. Here a former U. S. Marine took over 30 years ago when the land was on its knees from a hurricane and a revolution. Here he built his land without asking U. S. financial aid. That was good. That was bad, too.

I asked a friend, who must remain unnamed "How can travelers, diplomats, business men handle such figures as Gen-eral Trujillo, the former strong man with strong ideas, and win him over?"

"You must show sincerity and be friendly," was the simple answer.

"How, my friend?" I asked.

"First, when you talk to him, or about him, indicate friend-liness with smiles. The sincere smile is a universal sign of friendship. Then the person who may not fully see the mean-ing of your words, will feel from your smile that you are at least friendly and open minded. A smile goes a long way even with dictators who rule hard."

"Tell me other ways to win over iron men," I asked.

"You must be sympathetic to their views even though you disagree. When you disagree do so with a smile, not with an angry look. And when a strong one talks, nod your head even though you may inwardly disagree. For when it comes time to openly disagree, you have someone who is not hurt inwardly and will at least listen to you."

"Ah, I see. Then people often misunderstand us because of our attitude when we are talking or are listening."

"Precisely. Bend the head forward, lean toward the listener physically, even though you can't do so mentally. You disarm him that way. Then when you talk, talk simply—in the language he understands."

I saw what my friend meant. Here are some points anyone of us can apply to our daily contacts. You may wish to explode in disagreement. Don't. Listen well—listen friendly, then if you want to disagree, do so kindly.

It's truly an art to win over others.

CHAPTER THOUGHT

Be a good listener first—a good talker second.

WHEELERGRAMS TO FIT THE CHAIR TO THE PERSON—NOT THE PERSON TO THE CHAIR

Don't talk past people—look 'em in the eye.
"P" added to "luck" spells PLUCK.
Turn NOW backwards and it becomes WON.
Excel others—and you'll lose friends.
Beware of *detour* signs on bored friend's faces.

* * *

Work *with* people—not *on* them.
Be quick to agree—slow to disagree.

Slander, like coal, will dirty your own hand first.

2

If you want to become a success,
do so, but in the Jack Benny manner
of selling an image of yourself
that gets you across quickly
and easily with others

*"You cannot climb the ladder of success
with your hands in your pockets."*

I was in a good discussion with Rai Bahadu M. S. Oberoi of India.

This man is the Hilton of his fabulous land and we sat together; he, Dr. Brij Myer, Esther McEvoy Quiroz and myself, in one of the Oberoi suites in his Imperial Hotel in New Delhi.

India is a land of great truths, deep thought, and wonderful views of life, death and the ability of man to get along with mankind. So I put a question to Oberoi.

"This suite you call the Maharaja Suite," I said, "lives up to its image. I feel like a Maharaja."

I explained that my image of India was one of grandeur, opulence; of gilt and gold, silks and innumerable draperies; of turbaned sikhs and ever-present bearers, all catering to my every wish and making a fine picture of one's pre-conception of India.

"You mean you had an image of a hotel even before you arrived?" asked Oberoi.

I told him that the world does form images of places and people, and on going to the place or meeting the people the image either lives up, or down, to the anticipated daydreaming of the image seeker.

Oberoi sat thoughtfully back in a rounded, brocaded chair. He smiled as he mused for a moment, then said, "I see what you mean. We make images of ourselves to people, we do so either deliberately or subconsciously, and then people either buy our image or refuse. As a hotel man I perhaps have unconsciously made an image of myself and my hotels in the eyes of the world. How interesting, how interesting."

I turned then to Esther McEvoy Quiroz for she is the "image maker" of the Oberoi hotel chain. "You agree?" I asked.

"Indeed," she replied. "The world has two images of India: one of extreme poverty, one of the grandeur of the Maharaja. We prefer to sell the grandeur theme to travelers, and we seem to succeed."

At this point Dr. Myer said, "As a doctor, I must sell an image to my patients. I must sell them on my medical ability. I must sell them on my capabilities. I must sell them the fact that I am a worthy doctor for them to visit."

"How do you go about selling an image?" I asked. Dr. Myer thought a moment, then said:

"I give reflections of a professional man. That is what people buy and it includes reliability, confidence, respect and understanding."

"You mean that any person can sell an image of himself to others?"

"Yes, the doctor who doesn't appear like a doctor, may be an expert. Yet his lack of professionalism holds him back in life. Too often you get wrongful impressions of a practitioner who swears, dresses sloppy, even chews on cigars. Yet he is perhaps a good medical man. Today people prefer to buy images of a skilled technical man with a professional mannerism about him."

That then was the key-note of this discussion in India: that people buy images.

How People Buy "Images"

I thought of our talk in India many times. I thought of it just recently when I was watching a fiddle-player, Jack Benny. What image did this No. 1 comedian sell to the world?

One day I bumped into Jack's popular singer, Dennis Day. I put the image question to him and he said very quickly, "Jack does sell the world an image: it's penuriousness. He likes to make people think he is a cheap skate, yet the fellow is actually lavish with tipping."

Jack does sell this skin-flint image. I can remember when he was held-up in a scene in one of his TV programs and the hold-up man said, "Your money or your life." Jack hesitated . . . hesitated a long time, getting one of his biggest laughs in his career.

Benny, the image seller, puts across another idea about himself: his perennial age of 39. He is forever youthful, yet he's on the road to 70. He made the figure 39 symbolic with youth, as is the number 65 marks retirement from life. Jack once wanted to become 40 and announced on a TV program in advance when he'd have his 40th birthday. There were so many editorials written pleading that Jack not spoil the beautiful image he had given the world of perpetual youth, that the birthday party was cancelled.

What images do you want to sell to others?

Abraham Lincoln sold honesty. General Grant that of a cussin' general. Teddy Roosevelt promoted his image of a man with a big stick. So many people feel this is again needed these days in dealing quickly and firmly with foreign powers. Coolidge sold the world an image of New England thrift, and Rockefeller did the same with dimes—and the world bought all these images offered to them.

Let us agree then that people do buy images. That it's a wanted purchase, for they are saleable in any field you are in. The point is to find the right image to fit your work and your personality.

Frank Buck sold the image of a great African hunter by wearing a jungle hat. Will Rogers chewed gum, and had a knack of scratching his head as he stood on one foot, to sell an image of a government court jestor. Movie actors and actresses are all in the business of selling images—so we can safely conclude that an image of yourself can be sold. In fact, must be sold, if you are to get places in life.

Don't Sell Wrong Images

Diamond Jim Brady got a loan of diamonds from a pawn broker to enable him to reflect the image of prosperity as a salesman of railroad equipment. To be sure, the pawn broker wasn't too sold on the Brady scheme, so went along on the calls, "Just to protect my investment."

But you can project wrong images.

Hitler sold an image—but the world didn't buy it for long. So did Mussolini. So did Castro. So do many people on your own street sell images you won't buy. You recognize the expensive chrome-plated car to be beyond the income level of the owner. You don't buy the image of people who live beyond their status in life, putting on fronts and airs in an endeavor to portray someone they are not. You won't buy a phony image for long.

Beatniks sell images. So do advocates of off-brand doctrines.

How far do you think Castro would get once he shaved his beard? His vivid image would be lost to us, as well as to his barber.

Con men sell uranium stock by painting images of prosperity, or else their public would not buy. Thus the con man assumes the airs of the preacher, acts like the banker, and talks like the philanthropist—all to cover up his dishonesty! But unfortunately because he can't back up the image he ends up leaving for an extradition-free country—or the state prison.

Therefore, you must be cautious about the image you give to others.

Dr. Albert Edward Wiggam, a human relations writer, once said, "The biggest thing in education, in fact in all human life, is not selling things, but *selling yourself.*"

You must learn the art of selling yourself.

"She looks efficient," says the boss of the girl asking for a position. "I'll hire her."

How did this secretary sell the image of efficiency to the boss? No doubt through the way she walked into his office. For she walked in a direct, surefooted manner. She had an impressive walk. Then she sold her mode of dress, it was business-like, and her hair was neat. Next she smiled in a friendly way, answered questions in a crisp manner, and during a test of her ability to take dictation, she had a presharpened pencil ready, and a neat pad.

She sold herself as Miss Efficiency, an image any boss would buy.

Still that night at a party of friends, she sold another image: that of a neighborhood gal you'd like to know.

Her business-like dress had magically changed to one of feminine character, her hair hung loose now, and she handled her cocktail and cigarette in a confident manner with the finesse of a charming woman. And most important, she let the other person do most of the talking. We'll soon learn the effect that talking ten seconds and listening ten minutes has on potential husbands.

The girl had sold a business and a social image.

How?

Mainly because she had an image of herself to sell, for without pre-conceived ideas, a goal in life, a target to aim at, you can't develop images. You cannot form an image of something you haven't in mind. Therefore, Rule 1 in developing images is:

Know What You Want to Sell

Some of us sell our image naturally, for it fits in without make up. We don't need to sell an image of being rich if we are; nor do we need to sell an image of being beautiful, if we are. It is when we lack things that we must struggle to find proper images to get across to others, and at the same time divert others from our failings through focusing their attention on our strong features.

This is an important rule to remember.

You can lead people away from weak points, to strong points, if you have the proper tact, and this will be brought out to you along the way. But for the present, believe that you can lead people if you understand people and know what motivates them. Ralph Waldo Emerson and his son tried to motivate a calf to leave a stable. The father pushed—the son pulled. The calf balked. Then a passing servant put a finger into the calf's mouth, and led it from the stall.

You see you can lead if you are a leader.

Columbus was a leader of great explorations because he was able to sell the image to Queen Isabella that he was an explorer. She bought this image of Columbus: that he'd do something for her regime by discovering new lands and new ways to reach the riches of India. She financed him. But

Columbus had one other bit of sales psychology up his sleeve: he practiced "You—ability." By this he let the Queen see how she'd benefit, not what Columbus would gain. He talked "you," the world's biggest word, and not "I," the smallest word in any language.

As Adler, the noted psychologist put it, "Sell others the feeling of importance."

People buy that feeling.

3 Rules to Sell Images

Therefore, it behooves you:

1. To Know What You Want In Life.
2. To Find the Proper Image To Sell To Others.
3. To Back it Up With "You—ability."

That's three good rules to use in forming an image of yourself that will put you across with others, and help you go places in life.

"Look, Mom—No Hands"

Be warned: images can unsell as well as sell you.

Too often we unconsciously sell others an image of ourselves that is not true, and are forever after saying, "You don't understand me." That is because you projected a wrong image, as we will learn soon; but let me say now that people watch our way of walking, slouching, talking, eating, drinking, conversing—and form snap judgements. "You know, I always liked that person—somehow the way he walks impresses me." You will hear such remarks as that, or again, "Something about him annoys me." It is a remote radar signal that sends out messages to people and prompts them to like or dislike you at once. Often you get only ten seconds to make an effect on someone, so it is important to watch your first ten seconds with others.

And your first ten words are more important than your next 10,000.

Some people over-do the image making. A cute thing knows she's cute—and overly sells herself. An intellectual often goes too far in impressing others with his knowledge. A boy that is good on a bicycle is first to holler, "Look—no hands." But that is no way to win over people. No one likes a show off. No one warms up to a know it all. And the braggart gets faint applause when he shouts, "Look—no hands."

So don't kid yourself. Instead, be yourself.

People like normalcy in others. It makes them feel good to be among the average. People squirm in the presence of egg heads—even other egg heads squirm. The warm smile, the friendly attitude, does more to put you over than wisdom spouting forever from your brain. Talk with your heart—not your brain, and leave an image of yourself as a friendly cuss, not a learned bore.

"Know thyself" said Thales and many others after him; for in knowing yourself, good and bad, you learn how to suppress the bad and play up the good. "My right side photographs better," says the actor, not bragging, but just being sensible at the photographers. "That is something I know little about," says the worker, and gains respect from the boss for this frankness. We cannot be experts in everything. None of us are two-legged dictionaries. We are outstanding in something, fair in others, good in much, and bad in a lot. Just hide the bad—play up the good.

You gain the confidence of others when you use seven magic words and say: "That is something I know little about." It isn't a masterly phrase. It is not entirely good English—but it is good tact and diplomacy to admit the weak —and play up the strong, radiating a good image to others.

Seven little magic words to personal success.

Don't Be a Shy Guy

Once you are aware of your good points, stress them.

You cannot go around constantly bragging how good you are, but at the same time there is no need to hide your talents. Let the boss, friends, neighbors, relatives—the world —know you are a good salesman, bookkeeper, doctor or truck driver. Don't brag—just highlight your best features. Sell them to others, for it may be a long time before they find your hidden talents if you keep them under cover.

Don't be a shy-boy.

Attract subtle attention to your strength. Turn the best side forward.

But you can, take a weak point and make a strong point of it.

Martha Raye sold her big mouth to the world, just as Durante sold his elongated schnozzel. Eddie Cantor took a rasping voice and made it sing out; Herbert Hoover laughed very little, but sold the world on his engineering ability; Jack Benny sold horrible fiddle playing in the face of Heifetz, no less. Edison capitalized on his poor hearing by not hearing people criticize him by saying it couldn't be done; and Herbert Marshall, the actor with a wooden leg, became a lady's man because he handled himself in a distinguished manner.

We all have images to hide—images for sale.

I'd say that your initial step in any study of how to get along in the world is to find your image—then attract attention to it.

You'll go places if people have the right image of you.

CHAPTER THOUGHT

If you'd win a person to your cause, first sell him an image of you he'll buy. Then convince him you are what he thinks.

A LESSON IN ORIENTAL DIPLOMACY

**After the occupation of Japan, a general asked a notable
what he now thought about General MacArthur, and was told:
*"The Emperor couldn't have picked a better man!"***

3

It's no trick to make people feel like 30¢—
the trick is to make them feel
like a million dollars—
and here are some sizzling ways
to do it

> *"Respect is what we owe; love, what we give."*
> —Philip James Bailey

The Japanese, perhaps, have the softest sell of all nations. They move quickly, to be sure, and in a straight line, but with elegance, grace and courtesy, and with bows. They might teach us something in the art of making friends, so I asked Bill Turner of Tokyo for some ideas.

"When I started to live in Japan," he said, "I was impressed with Japanese courtesy even in the heat of business transactions. It exuded a sort of comfort to me, and invariably made me respond and become polite. You cannot bow to another without that person wanting to bow back."

"Courtesy then makes one feel like a million dollars?"

"Yes, being polite brings out the good in others. The Japanese makes his bows in proportion to the reverence he wants to give. A slight bow for the casual acquaintance. Deeper for friends. Way down for one he highly reveres."

"I see what you mean," I said. "Americans are inclined to express their respect for others through the length of hand pumping which often is over done to an irritating point. Europeans are softer, too, on their handshake," I added, "usually one soft up and down, maybe two pumps. Latin Americans never go in for hand pumping, or back slapping. They do embrace fond friends and dear ones, I've observed, but never do they overly-pump one another's hand."

We had been sitting in the lobby of the New Imperial Hotel with its impresario, Tetsuzo Inumara, and Iwao Yokota, of the Japan Tourist Association, who said, softly, "May I be so brave as to pass on a word of information?" We nodded to this man who serves so many thousands of visitors each year. His words are wisdom, itself. He said:

"We in Japan never take liberty to tell a person he is wrong. We always excuse ourselves for not understanding what he has said. We invite him to talk further on his subject of question, and often we find it unnecessary to contradict. He talks himself into his own answers."

I thought that over a moment, for you always must think over oriental statements to fully appreciate their every meaning and nuance.

Then Turner said, "I see what Iwao means. I can remember Harry Baldwin of New York who once told his Japan Airline ticket sellers never to say the customer was wrong, but to assume they did not fully understand the customer and would he be so kind as to repeat his statement. In repeating, often the customer corrects his error or modifies his thinking and less harm is done than would be if the seller contradicted the customer. This is mighty good strategy in getting along with people."

It sounded sensible to me.

Only too often I have heard someone say, "You are wrong. Now listen to me." How much better if he'd responded in the oriental fashion and said, "I am sorry I didn't quite understand you. Can you please explain further?"

The same goes for explanations. You are quick to say, "You didn't understand what I said." This upsets the other person. It is calling him stupid.

How much better to use the gentle sell and say, "I am sorry I did not make myself clear enough. What I meant to say was . . ." This gives the other person a chance to save his face.

And it certainly saves your own face.

Jasmine Chan's Secret

I asked Major Henry Stanley of Hong Kong, who guides merchants in their handling of tourists, what ideas he may have to make a person feel like a million dollars. We were sitting in the tea lounge of the Hotel Carlton high over Hong Kong. The Major took his eyes off the spectacular scenery of the harbor long enough to say, "I think one way to make a person feel good is to use his name. It is an oriental trait I like. Especially when the first name can be used."

"But suppose it is a difficult name, then what?" I countered.

"Then take a moment, as we British do, and be sure you have it correct. Nothing offends more than mispronouncing a person's name. I often quietly ask the correct pronunciation of others' names before I use them on their owners. I find this makes lasting friends."

"Suppose no one is around to ask the correct pronunciation of a name?"

"Then I ask the person, himself, for the proper pronunciation."

"Doesn't this embarrass him?" I asked.

"On the contrary, it flatters that person. It elevates his ego to know I would like to learn how he pronounces his name properly."

At this point Rudy Choy and Miss Jasmine Chan came to the table. We all stood to be introduced. And as we shook hands (for the Chinese shake hands rather than bow), I asked each their ideas of how to make people feel like a million dollars.

Jasmine Chan said: "I make friends by giving six calling cards to each visitor in my shop."

"Calling cards—six of them to a customer?" we all exclaimed, indicating our perplexity of her Chinese system of friend-making.

"Yes," said Jasmine. "On each card I write, 'Jasmine wants to see you.' I invite my customers, usually from far places in the world, to send their friends to see me and drink with me—and you know, I get an average of 2 cards back per customer. It is a great way to make people feel important for they show up with the cards and at once feel at home with me."

We all nodded in agreement at Jasmine's system of making friends for her late husband's wholesale liquor establishment which she now operated.

3 Ways to Remember Names

Hong Kong is the world's greatest general store, since it is a free port. So when the Marco Polo Restaurant proprietor gave me a lighter with a tape measure that pulled from its bottom, I observed an oriental way to make friends—for all day long people are buying things in Hong Kong, and measuring this, that and the other thing. It was an appropriate friend-maker, of good ingenuity, and a conversation piece that made the owner feel happy with his unusual gift.

Perhaps around you are such unusual gifts. Things that don't smack of a free give-away merely to gain business. It is more important at first to gain goodwill from what is given others, than to gain monetary advantages.

*

Perhaps the best of all the ways to make people feel like a million dollars is to practice Major Stanley's idea of using people's names, so here are three ways to remember them:

1. *Hear the Name*
    You can't remember what you don't hear. If you fail to hear the name, do as recommended by Major Stanley, and ask the other person to repeat it—for you elevate that person's ego.

2. *Repeat the Name*
    In so doing you impress it deeply on your memory muscles. Too often we say "sir" and "madam" in our business dealings, and fail to impress the name on our memory muscles. But if you use the name constantly during a conversation, it has remembrance value.

3. *Associate the Name*
    And the more ridiculous the association, the easier it will be to recall it weeks, months, even years later. You meet Mr. Pickeltwister and say to yourself. "Mr. Pickeltwister —he twists pickles in a pickle factory." You meet Mrs. Henrietta, and you say over and over to yourself, "A hen that is always ready." That's the trick to remember people's names.

I think one's name is more important to that person in winning him to your way of thinking, than any other way I know. It makes people feel important. A VIPI—a very important person *indeed!*

Singapore Freddie's System

Another subtle oriental way to make people feel good, is side-step use of negatives. As explained to me one day in Singapore by Freddie Eu:

"I try to hide from others any worries or unhappiness I may have. Long ago I found that to tell people of my troubles made them unhappy. So I wear a false face of happiness, even on days when I am down and blue. Soon the happiness of others practicing this same oriental trick, gets me out of my doldrums. I become a happy man, too."

I see what Freddie means. For I have seen people try to win over others by saying, "I don't suppose I could interest you in going to the affair Saturday, could I?" That is putting the "no" reply right in their mouths. Far better to be positive and say, "I *know* you will want to go along Saturday. *You'll be missed* if you don't go."

That elevates the other person. Makes him important.

It is never wise to speak negatively, but to phrase your language in positive ways: "Knowing the person you are, I know this is something you'll want to do." That excites interest. Makes it easier to get yourself across with others faster, and get favorable responses.

Try being positive—not negative.

*

The trick is to lead with a leading question—not your chin!

*

Don Wilson, an airline sales manager in New York City, who often frequents foreign lands, has learned a trick to make waiters feel like a million dollars.

"I always find something to compliment the waiter. Maybe the salad. Maybe the coffee. But something I can say, as I leave, that was unusually good that day. Even though he had nothing to do with the cooking, he likes the compliment. It raises his spirits. He is better for the rest of the day. And, of course, on my return he is all smiles *for me.*"

*

How few times we compliment the help.

How little we pass on a kind word to the worker. But if we do, we win over that person . . . and get better service.

Next time you are paying your check, tell the waiter something nice about the meal, horrible as it may have been.

You'll be doing *yourself* a lot of good!

A Method From Peru

Eduardo Arrarte of Peru often deals with American visitors in his land. One day I remarked about the way his customers, mostly women, seemed so friendly to him. I asked, "What is your big secret of making people, especially women, feel like a million dollars?"

He said, "I am quick to observe something they might have just purchased, and I compliment it. Perhaps it is only a scarf, a shawl, or perhaps even a dress. And even if it is not new, the person beams all over for my observation. It makes them feel good . . . and it makes me rich!"

Too often the wife brings a new dress home. Silently she parades it in front of hubby, who fails to observe it. Finally she shouts, *"Don't you notice anything new about me today?"*

He eyes her up and down. "Curled your hair different?" he asks, feebly.

"No, you big so and so—it's my new dress!" she shouts.

He mutters, "Oh, is it *new?*"

But suppose he had been alert to such things. Quick to say, "You've a new dress." Her ego would be inflated. She'd feel like a millionairess—and the old boy's dinner would have been cooked even better.

Be observant of others and quick to note their new possessions. That's how to be a millionaire: by making others feel like one.

In so doing you make lasting friends. Enrich your soul and your purse!

*

Don't take people for granted!

How Cemetery Sellers Sell

Making people happy at weddings is no trick; but at funerals, that is another question.

Larry Doyle of Forest Lawn Memorial Park in Los Angeles, tells me of his secret to alleviate pain and sorrow. "We treat every person as if he were our own kin folk. We serve each person as if he were a close member of our own family. This gains the respect of people. They even give us smiles of thank you in the very midst of their bereavement."

Too often we deal with others in a cold manner. To be sure, they are buying from us, but that is no reason they should be treated like mechanical pocketbooks. So open up. Relax. Smile. Be cheerful.

You'll get a faster response with warmth than cold.

Make your regular customers as much family friends as possible, rather than business bank books.

*

Look at others' qualities—not their checking accounts.

*

"The only true source of politeness is consideration," claims William Gilmore Simms, the noted writer.

Politeness breeds politeness—just as Japanese bows breed bows. But one warning:

Be sure your courtesy and politeness and concern for others is real. Genuine. Not something you mutter absentmindedly as you say on greeting people, "How are you?" You'd be aghast if that person started to explain how he actually felt that day!

Most people know, "How are you?" is a passing salutation not to be taken seriously. But these same people do want to take you seriously when you go deeper into their lives, perhaps saying, "I'd like your advice on this matter."

People can detect honest sincerity.

They are keen to separate the insincere words of people, from the sincere remark.

You must have a genuine regard for others, to reflect sincerity. A flippant, "You look adorable today," is taken lightly by the woman, especially when that is a known favorite remark of the flatterer. An admiring smile from another is often more genuine to her than a pompous bit of put-on flattery.

Voltaire's Winning Technique

Another rule is to avoid sweet-talking people.

As Voltaire put it so aptly. "We cannot always oblige, but we can always speak obligingly."

You cannot always accept the thinking of others, but you can respect their freedom to think as they choose. You can neither challenge their feelings on their religion, politics, nor some important national side-taking issue such as segregation versus integration. Each person has a right to his own side. That is what makes Republicans and Democrats. What keeps the free world on a straight course, for if everybody rowed up the same river, no new rivers in life would be discovered. Welcome the other person's thinking. Add it to your own. But never be unobliging enough to say negatively, "I don't agree."

*

An ancient proverb says, "We must go to people to see what they are like."

*

But no proverb ever said we must bluntly disagree with their views or side taking. Nor can "a man without a smiling face open up a shop." He must be agreeable to get along in life, making others feel like millionaires. The "truth is often the strongest argument," say the gentle orientals; so speak what you believe is the truth, and let others accept or not as they choose. That is their perogative.

Two people, thinking this way, can argue like a man of Naples, providing they finally lock arms, as does the Neapolitan after the argument, and go merrily on in friendship.

*

Remember, you can't fool all of the people all of the time —but someone is always trying.

Don't you be that someone!

*

Politeness of others always makes me feel like a million dollars, if I sense the politeness is sincere.

Mr. Peppe's is a dining place in Dallas that makes me feel elated, not only from the food but the politeness of papa (the cook) and mama (the maestro). Their Swiss politeness brings politeness out in me, for politeness is catching.

And I react to this Swiss couple by always thanking each for something particular served that night so politely, and I, in return, make them feel, too, like a million dollars.

But this all must be done sincerely.

*

The big trick in being sincere is: *talk from the heart.*

When the heart flows, so does sincerity.

Sure You Are Right?

But when the mind thinks up cute and clever things to say, bon mots of the moment, others don't take you sincerely. They can almost see your mind working to manufacture smart sayings to impress others, or to concoct false flattery to fool others. There is a difference between mental bits of thought-up flattery, and the true compliment that sincerely flows from the heart. As Hugh Blair once said, "Nothing except what flows from the heart can render external manners truly pleasing."

You will go further in life saying, "I am sorry" than "You are wrong."

It gives others a lift when you say, "I guess I am in error," than to say, "Are you sure you are right?" Give people a chance to save their ego!

*

Don't make people feel like 30 cents!

*

Another trick to make someone feel like a million dollars, is to give him an important assignment.

This will not only fill him with a sense of self importance but will also serve to bring out the best in him. Often there are qualities of real leadership lying dormant in people that only come to the surface when responsibility is suddenly shifted to their shoulders.

By giving persons important assignments you will find that they will put their excess energy to work *for you,* not against you.

I have observed this tactic at PTA meetings and at civic clubs, where those doing the most objecting, are often given the biggest assignments to do something. It flatters their ego —for often their loud objection is only to gain the recognition that we so want in life. When recognized and given a Chief's assignment instead of an Indian's job, that person is happy.

Try giving important responsibility to those around you. Make them feel important. Raise their ego. You'll have a millionaire around you in short order.

*

The horse whip has gone out of style.

*

A pastor I know wanted a certain person to attend church more often. All the usual appeals failed, for golf had a greater lure. Then one day the philosophical preacher said, "Joe, I've a big assignment that only you can do. No one else can do it. But it means church every Sunday for you. Will you make it?"

Flattered, the sudden "millionaire" started to be a church regular.

He had an important assignment now each Sunday. It made him feel important—far more than on the golf course, where often three other men made him feel like 30 cents!

CHAPTER THOUGHT

You'll cause less damage if you raise your eyebrows, rather than the roof.

SELF-MADE RULES FOR SELF-MADE PEOPLE
—AND ALL OTHERS

1. Remember people's names, and use them—pronouncing them the way *they* like.
2. Encourage others to talk, so you can be a good listener.
3. Be honestly sincere with others, especially when you compliment them.
4. Always talk in the language of the other person, for this makes him feel important.
5. Talk to people about—themselves!
6. Think twice—speak once, maybe not at all.
7. Discuss—never argue.
8. Talk weddings—not funerals.

4

How an inferiority complex
saps your energy, drains pep,
loses friends—and what
you can do about it

"All fearfulness is folly."

"Whenever I have a feeling of being inferior, I put a cigar
in my mouth, the longer the cigar the better I feel."

So said Bob Boyd of Panama to me one day as we were
watching the sun set in the Atlantic after having seen it rise
that morning in the Pacific. That sight, hind-end, was
enough to give anyone a feeling of inferiority, and I told this
to Boyd who is an official greeter of people visiting this
country. Boyd laughed.

"Yes," he said, "and if you'd see the square tree trunks we
have around here, gold colored frogs—and later on farther
south see smoke curl up counter-clockwise, and water going
backwards down drains, you'd surely end up with a big feeling of inferiority—for lack of knowledge often gives one that
feeling."

"You mean a person with little education feels inferior in
front of those well educated?"

"In a way—until that person suddenly sees he is greatly superior to the other person in many other respects. For we are all *stupidos* on many subjects while learned on others. It is when you pity yourself, or fear for your pride and self-being, that you get a case of the inferiorities and run to dark corners to hide."

I thought Boyd put it quite well.

I have seen women feeling inferior but upon buying a dress, become an extrovert again. I have seen people wiggle conversations around to what they excel in, and change from a bashful person to a bold one.

"A red purse bolsters my ego," claims a lady friend. "It gives me a lift."

There must be many big "cigars" and many "red purses" in your life to bolster your ego; if you search them out and learn the art of imparting these good points to others, you won't remain hidden behind a bushel basket or under a palm in the far corner of the dance floor.

Mankind has many ways to raise his ego.

Elsa Maxwell was born on the wrong side of the railroad tracks, and developed a beautiful inferiority complex as a child when she didn't have a new party dress, and was severely high-hatted by the rich girl who refused to invite her to a party. What did Elsa do? Nothing much except to get durned mad and become the world's greatest party thrower!

That's how she blasted her inferiority complex!

Cass Daley had buck teeth in the days when children didn't go to dentists to have them straightened. So she smiled very little for fear others would laugh at her buck teeth. Then one day she, too, like Elsa, got mad. She became determined to lift herself by her boot straps, and did. She became a movie actress. So did Jimmy Durante win out by a nose; and Martha Raye by a big mouth; and Joe E. Brown won out with a big yell from what he called a "hole in my head; my mouth."

Nature wasn't kind to these people, but nature also provided them with an urge to overcome nature's handicap: *nature gave these people a will to win.*

Atlas Overcame Defeat

It seems that people born with a handicap have an extra gift of strength of will inside them. Nature takes care of people that way. The blind hear better; the deaf see better. The poor have goals ahead. It's all the Great Law of Compensation that makes up for a weakness with an extra strength somewhere else.

The great body builder, Atlas, was born with a weakling's body. Arthur Murray, the dance pro, was a skinny lad who became the life of the party.

Yet both overcame nature's handicaps. Both succeeded because they made up their minds to achieve success.

The Texas "Poor Boy"

There was Jack Marvin of Texas, for example, who put it this way: "I was not only born with a cleft lip, but a gold spoon. I got over my speech difficulty quickly, but that golden spoon handicap nearly got me down."

For it weakened Marvin. It robbed him of an urge. There was no need for the little rich boy to have a goal in life to aim at. He had all the gold spoons he could use.

Today Jack still has gold—but of his own making. He has oil. He has fingers in many businesses, including a new island he "discovered" in the Caribbean that he is bringing back to life. "The island was rich in resources, so it had little reason to get moving anymore than I did," explained Marvin. "But I'm showing the people there how to extend themselves, bring in the outside world. Perhaps this may be harmful, but we have a plan to put the island on the map—and to maintain its character."

Marvin, the poor little rich boy, has made good.

Don't Hide Handicaps

Most inferiority complexes begin with worry.

The person worries that he is no good, lacking, not up to standard in some way, and he becomes a bashful boy or a shy girl, sitting in the dark corners of life instead of out front on the big porch where the passing world can see.

Then something takes hold of that shy and bashful kid. Maybe it is a little whispering they heard behind their backs; maybe it is a sudden realization that we are all rich in some respect, and must sell that richness to hide the poverty in us. For our lack, remember, gives us strength.

Steinmetz went far in life despite a twisted body.

Edison was hard of hearing. It held him back until suddenly he realized, "I am lucky. I hear only what I want to hear."

That point of view thrust him forward in life. It opened doors for him. Today it is fashionable to wear a hearing device. It makes people appear distinguished, not dumb. Bernard Baruch wears one in public. So does Herbert Hoover, Jr. And a singer named Johnny Ray.

None hide it—for it makes them proud!

Beware of Your Dreams

Pasteur is another who overcame parental backwardness to emerge a success; for once you determine to go places, nothing can stop your will to win.

As was said: "Beware of what you will, for you will get it!"

FDR wanted to be president of the U. S., and despite polio, won this highest office we can offer anyone in the U. S. The other Roosevelt, Teddy, was a weakling. He had to be sent out West for a lung ailment. He fought it successfully. Ended up famous by charging up San Juan Hill and becoming president of the country. Bad health can at first seem a handicap; but once you overcome it, you are stronger than all the others around you.

Debbie Drake's Story

A salesman with flat feet bemoaned his handicap. He felt worse than a singer with a throat ailment.

But the salesman had a will. He reached for the telephone instead of a walking stick, and made his calls that way.

When Debbie Drake, the gorgeous TV exercise girl, was a teenager she was a scrawny, curveless, self-conscious kid with few friends or dates. But she decided to do something about it. She read everything she could find on diet and exercise. She exercised for hours every day. Her figure blossomed. Today she is television's number one physical fitness queen, appears on 70 TV stations and is in the $100,000 a year income bracket.

Now that's something, isn't it!

Ways to Detect Inferiorities

How can you detect a big case of the inferiorities?

In many ways—namely in the over-quiet, sitting in rear of school rooms, back rows of sales meetings, last seats in church. Other signs that give shyness away are:

- Being last to queue up
- Last to be served at a buffet

- Last to raise a hand in a class or meeting
- Walking always behind others
- Blushing too easily—and often
- A weak hand-shake
- Listening too much, talking too little
- An eye that won't meet another's eye
- Book worms
- Anyone in any dark corner
- An umbrella carrier with rain coat
- A soft-toned talker

Look around you. You'll see many such give-aways of one who is overly shy and needlessly bashful, who nurses a fear he is inferior to others, has little to offer at gatherings, sales meetings; who sits in rear seats so as not to be called upon; who is always last in line ups and who hates to look others directly in the eye.

One tip off, strangely, that you are inwardly scared is over-talking!

People who are scared often talk too much.

But it is apt to be a babble of nothing—for they are merely trying to cover up their supposed weakness or handicap with a lot of conversation. That person is often truly fearful of his inferiorities.

*

Tip: don't be fooled by overly-avid conversationalists!

*

An extrovert is often born that way through hopped-up glands.

Nature gave him "go." He has great energies, and these physical attributes of birth give him lots of energy. He is bouncy and bounding. He is a lucky person, providing he can harness this great energy and put it to useful work.

Eleanor Roosevelt is an example of that type. Even today she bounds around the world. Walter Reuther is that way, despite his arm injury received during early union activity. Grandma Moses and Churchill, of course, show what great body strength these lucky ones can use to keep up in life.

Such extroverts, lacking in inferiorities, are stimulating to associate with.

But certain others are not.

These are the extroverts that extrovert too loud and too often. They are too much the life of the party. The practical jokers. The over-talkers. The dominant ones trying to dominate. These might be such as Peron, Trujillo, Castro, Hitler —and Russians who try to hide their inferiority by being boastful and loud voiced, until some little fellow with guts shows them up for what they truly are: hopped-up extroverts!

At first these super-extroverts give others a lift. We admire their great push. This eggs them on even further and gives them false feelings of grandeur. Soon they go beyond the call of "go"; and are soon taken care of by those around them.

The weed that grew so fast and so strong, soon finds someone has developed a weed killer!

You Can't Pick Parents

Woodrow Wilson was a Princeton grad. That's as hard to overcome in life as getting all A's at Harvard. Success can be a great handicap in the wrong hands. Wilson got over his diploma. So did President Eisenhower with rare West Point training. On the other hand, President Truman pulled himself up from his own low beginning to become a president. He was certainly no "egg head." And today he still out-walks reporters at 6:00 a.m.

So you can let your up-bringing help or hinder you.

You can take a humble beginning in life and make it end

in grandeur; or you can be born in grandeur, and end up unknown in life. A snook.

It all lies in your desires and goals in life.

It is said, "Pick your parents for long life." That may be true. But if Atlas and Teddy Roosevelt and Cass Daley and Durante can make the grade in life despite their handicaps, so can you.

*

Harpo Marx had no charming voice. So he learned to be a comic with a wig and a bicycle horn. And he also learned to play the harp!

*

People who strut diplomas get no place in life.

It is fine to earn a Phi Beta Kappa key—and to wear it—but not on your lapel. It loses friends by making people feel inferior in your presence.

*

Beware of the person who drives an old Ford. He may be able to afford a Rolls-Royce!

"The full teapot," says an ancient proverb, "makes no sound."

Statler always warned his reservation clerks in his hotels: "Beware of the man from over the hills."

One day a man came into his early St. Louis Statler, blew dust off his clothes, and asked for a room. The clerk took one look at the beragged individual and put him into a rear low-priced room. The fellow got mad. He asserted himself, identified himself—and with bows was quickly placed into the Presidential suite. He was the man from "over the hills" with no false pretenses, no reasons to flaunt his great wealth.

When Mrs. Jack Johnson, mother of the great boxer, once

walked into Macy's to buy a rug, all the salesmen deliberately overlooked her, waiting for someone who looked like they could buy expensive rugs. But not one seller. He approached her and ended up with a $1,000 order!

Beware of people who drive ancient Fords!

A Good Trick to Use

We all fear the laughter of others.

Such fear gives us giant size inferiorities. That's the reason for this greatest of advertisements: "They Laughed When I Sat Down at the Piano, But When I Started to Play Their Glances Turned to Ones of Admiration." This headline, in various forms, has sold more pianos than any similar appeal.

"Do You Make These Mistakes in English," is another all time successful ad, appealing to most of us who fear the embarrassment of making grammatical errors in English in front of others.

If you wish to raise the sense of power inside of others, *recognize them.*

That's a big secret of getting one over his inferiority complex.

We are all hungry for recognition. We all want the kind of glances of others, the verbal praises. We are thirsty for recognition. Give it to people, and in return they'll give you their respect—and business.

Listen for Opportunity

And remember, we are all superior in something.

I can't add 2 and 2 and get 4. So I let others do this book-keeping for me, those who excel in this while I go about trying to excel in something that appeals more to me.

The trick to turn an inferiority into a superiority complex?
First: *know wherein you excel!*
Second: *don't hide yourself behind a bushel basket.*
Let the world know wherein you are outstanding. Sell this
to the world. Keep selling it. Someday someone will find you
just as they found Lana Turner in a Hollywood drug store.
Be always prepared for the knock of opportunity.
Many a movie star today started as another star's stand-in.
Then came the time the star got restless, hard to handle, sick,
or lazy. The stand-in had his chance and was "discovered,"
as you will be discovered some day if you are constantly pre-
paring yourself for that Moment of Truth when the world
suddenly "sees" you for the first time.
Finding your strong, excel-points in life, is the best trick
I know to overcome an inferiority complex. As the oriental
puts it, "Do not peddle wood in the forest . . . or sell fish
by the lake shore."
To change conversation to subjects wherein you are expert,
is a stunt practiced by alert people who want to get into the
whirl of social or commercial conversation.
This is the best way I know to change from a wall flower
to a conversation tiger!

A Chinese Secret

"Pick your inn before the dark—get out on your road before the dawn," is a Chinese success secret.
What is education anyway?
Charlie Goodyear had little formal schooling, yet when a
glob of rubber fell to a hot stove lid and vulcanized itself, he
was educated enough to see how this phenomenon could
make tires. Brainy, educated scientists didn't have the "education" to see this.
O'Sullivan liked to walk on a "pad of rubber" as he

worked at his bench. He felt others might like the same feeling. That was an educated mind working. Now we all wear rubber heels.

A boy gets tired of peeling potatoes for his mother—so he invents a potato peeler. Was this education? Yes, but not formal. But all husbands, and GI's, think the lad was certainly *highly* educated!

A fellow sees natives whirling hoops around their waists. He brought the idea to America, and sold it as the Hula Hoop craze and made thousands of dollars. Is he educated . . . or not?

College degrees don't promise such braininess.

Dick Hartley tells of a man in London who sold train tickets around Europe; he could only sell tickets just to the next country. Here the traveler had to buy other tickets and gamble on the availability of seats. This thinker wondered, why not make available a ticket that would take a traveler clear through to his journey's end? He sold the idea all over Europe. Everyone liked it. The idea caught on . . . and so did Thomas Cook & Son!

Cook had a brainy idea and sold it!

*

If people won't dance to your tune, find a tune they'll dance to. That is what Arthur Murray did when no one danced with him as a boy. Now we all go to him to learn how to dance.

CHAPTER THOUGHT

"That man who knows too many trades, his family starves."
—Chinese proverb

A Short Short Story

You'll Make People Happy By This One Simple Rule

The rule is:

Give kindness when it is not expected!

The surprise value of unexpected acts of kindness wins others over faster than any other way I know.

When kindness comes from an unexpected source, or comes unsolicited from someone, it rings like a thousand cathedral bells. It boomerangs, making you feel good in return.

The person who lets you pass in front of his car gets the glad hand. The person who stands aside to permit you to enter a business doorway first gets the business—and a door opened for himself in return.

It is the unexpected kindness that counts most in life.

So go out this very day and be kind to someone not demanding it, not expecting it. Stand aside to let someone pass in front of you. It's a great way to start the day.

You'll feel better when someone gives you a kind smile, a friendly look, or a grateful glance in return for your unexpected show of kindness. That's a "thank you" your money cannot buy.

So be selfish—make a kind gesture to someone and get one in return.

Start a Kindness Week!

"Hide your offended heart—keep your valued friends."

5

How to harness an inferiority complex
and make it work overtime for you
in getting you down
the road to your daydreams

"Vision is the art of seeing things invisible."—Swift

So you have an inferiority complex!

Thousands do, too, but don't realize it.

You feel uncomfortable with people; you shy into dark corners; you are a bashful youngster and this is holding you back.

But is it holding you, and hundreds of others, back in life?

Lincoln and Alexander the Great had oversize inferiority complexes that they overcame. So did Norman Vincent Peale.

Look around you at successful people, and you may be surprised, upon close investigation, to observe they had to overcome an inferiority complex early in life before they went down the highway to success.

Giannini, founder of the great Bank of America in California, helped finance the Golden Gate Bridge when all others shied away. He once sold vegetables from a huckster's wagon in our Land of Opportunity—and had a bad case of the inferiorities, but soon got over it.

Superman an Introvert?

Freud discovered the inferiority complex, plus other things.

And he had himself as his own best student, for he had an inferiority complex.

He soon saw that a complex is "an unconscious repressed system of desires," and he set about to analyze complexes pro and con.

He observed that the person with a bigger car than yours, finer clothing, and the biggest house in town, was often overcoming some form of inferiority complex and was using this means to bolster himself.

People who talk too loudly, dominating conversations, are often people with inferiority complexes trying hard to assert themselves.

Many men who smoke over-size cigars were once poor and use the cigar as a status symbol.

Superman perhaps was once a dunce. But overcame his inferiorities, and became an extrovert instead of a quiet introvert as often happens when a Milquetoast in life suddenly feels his oats and tears loose from his complex.

That's the complexities of an inferiority complex.

Psychology of Cigar Smoking

A person who smokes the dollar-size cigar has a different personality than the person who smokes the more quiet looking fifteen cent Panatella size. Many extrovert actors smoke those giant size cigars. It seems to shout "success." The banker is more apt to smoke the neater Panatella shapes, since he has the money, knows it, and smokes just because the cigar tastes good to him.

Could Jimmy Corral, the cigar maker of Tampa, say that the bigger the cigar the bigger the inferiority complex someone is trying to overcome? As an example, Castro! Never seen without a giant size cigar in his beard.

But how about Winston Churchill? Could you say sometime back in his life he had an inferiority complex? Were his long cigars once an attempt to sell himself to others, until the cigar became such a trade-mark for him that he had to continue the show?

Adler's Three Points

Dr. Alfred Adler took issue with Freud. He claimed if an individual understood his inferiority complex, it could be easily corrected. That, unlike what Freud claimed, it wasn't always a sex deprivation; that such a complex wasn't always of neurotic nature. *Often it was just failure to attain a goal.*

Adler felt, to lack a complex, would in fact be abnormal. That to have an inferiority complex was important; that you then had something to "handle," and you could use the complex as one uses a diving board.

Adler gave this formula to overcome a complex:

1. First admit you have a complex.
2. Recognize its symptoms in others.
3. Use your complex as a springboard.

I Will Overcome My Handicap

In her book, *The Importance of Feeling Inferior* (Harper), Marie Bynon Ray points out many people in life who have had an inferiority complex, yet mastered it and have gone on to success.

In part she names El Greco, the painter, who had eye troubles; Mozart and Beethoven with aural handicaps; Jules Verne, Goethe and Milton with visual defects. Yet each in turn whipped his handicap and the inferiority complex it gave him, and went into extraordinary success in a field where physically he was the weakest.

Their weakness made them strong.

All know the great orator, Demosthenes, and how he had to put pebbles in his mouth to overcome a stutter. Jack Paar, the star of the late hour TV show also mastered this difficulty. Harold Maynard of Texas sells Webcor musical instruments, yet he has what he calls a "tin ear."

But each had one motto: *"I will overcome my handicap."*

See Only Outstanding Qualities

One trick to overcome a handicap is to: *See only my outstanding qualities.*

I can't be good in all things, but in those I am good in, I'll call to my attention constantly.

To do this, concentrate on your good points and belittle your weaknesses—in fact, put your complex into the trash can. *Can it!*

Henley said, "I am master of my fate; I am the captain of my soul."

You, too, are . . . captain of your life.

For a complex is merely a point of view. Look at your weak legs, and you will get nowhere in life. But if, as did Juan Belmonte, the matador, you forget your weak legs and learn how to direct the bull with a cape, then you are highlighting your good qualities and hiding the weak.

So maybe Rule One to overcome a complex is: *Learn To See Only The Good Things In Which You Excel.*

Capitalize on Your Weakness

A good general will analyze the situation, his particular situation. He knows where he excels, where he is weak—and acts accordingly.

He puts his best foot (or cannon) forward. In so doing, he covers up his deficiencies so the enemy sees only the sword and cannon aimed at him, and responds accordingly.

Nations are always bluffing one another. The Russians are expert at the game of bluff. Here is where our government is weakest.

Babe Ruth had more strike outs than home runs. But upon his failures he built his success.

Al Capp, of L'il Abner fame, had a wooden leg. He didn't become a track star, but a star cartoonist. Few knew of his bad leg. All knew of his cartoons.

Jimmy Durante had the big nose; Martha Raye the big mouth along with Joe E. Brown, yet all became movie stars. They didn't hide their facial features, but sold them to the public, making them their symbol and their trade mark.

In these particular cases, these people didn't hide their weakness, but brought it into the light of success.

And that might be Rule Two: *Play Up The Weakness!*

Killing Your Inferiority

At first this sounds silly—to play up your weakness. It's the opposite to Rule One—to hide the weakness. Yet it wasn't silly for stars who made fortunes by capitalizing on their handicaps of birth.

"I play lousy golf," said a friend of mine, "but I have fun at it." He didn't make any attempt to hide his poor golf. He played it up; and in so highlighting it, he made light of his bad scores.

Drew Pearson, the columnist, to me is a poor speaker; but a good writer. Fulton Lewis, Jr. is a good speaker, but a poor writer. Each has highlighted his good point, slighting over his inferior ones.

Bernarr Macfadden and Sandow, both symbols of physical prowess, were not strong men to start with. Each was a weakling, and each overcame his handicap, and went on to become a symbol of mighty biceps.

Each killed his inferiority.

So did Atlas, another "strong man." Charles Atlas was also born puny, but always admired Greek statues. They became a fetish for the thin little boy. One day Atlas said he'd become strong, too, like the Greeks in the statues, and he won out.

Will Rogers couldn't sing or dance worth a darn. He was a failure. He knew his weakness. He knew, too, people liked his wise-cracks he often made to kill time on the stage. One day he decided to stop his poor singing and dancing, and merely wise-crack on politics. Well, you know the success this brought him.

The Napoleonic Complex

If a person is born superior, he has no handicap to overcome: nor any goal to reach.

This may give him the frustrations that wealthy sons and daughters often inherit, similiar to those of the children of famous people, who are also subjected to the wealth and limelight of their families. This is indeed a handicap, but many have overcome it.

The Rockefellers and the Fords are good examples. There are many bad examples of others in the newspaper headlines of the various escapades that occupy the time of rich men's sons and daughters. They have too much freedom and no knowledge of how to use it properly.

Elsa Maxwell wasn't born rich, but on the wrong side of the railroad tracks, and no one invited her to parties. She had no clothes for parties. But this didn't give her the inferiorities. She later made a fetish of parties as Atlas did of Greek statues, and you know what she became in life: the "party girl" for kings and queens. She made a profession of "throwing parties" for wealthy people who would never have invited her to their homes when she was an underprivileged child.

James Barrie, points out Marie Beynon Ray, was just slightly over five feet tall. This worried him no end. He got a tall size complex over his miniature size.

He was ashamed of his stature, and seldom appeared in public; yet he didn't turn into a Napoleonic braggart as do so many short people who feel they are overcoming their small size with big Napoleonic struts.

In fact, Barrie gave the world Peter Pan—the story of a person who could entertain others in fantastic flights of fiction. No doubt this was the image Barrie saw for himself!

The Short and Long of It

Many short-statured dictators have become Napoleonic in life. You will note how they cultivate high military hats, to make them look taller—and in public they douse their breast with many medals, just to hide their feeling of inferiority, and to emphasize instead their sense of self-importance.

One firm does a land office business these days with so-called elevator shoes, designed to add height to short people, to give them the feeling of importance so desired by people.

For like a small dog who finds his bark scares bigger dogs,

a person suddenly gaining a little height from tall-boy shoes, also overcomes his introverted fears. Often he develops terrific cases of ultra-importance. Many dictators and gangsters do just that, until they are brought down to size by machine gun bullets.

One way to knock the bluff out of these Napoleonic characters is to make light of their strutting.

Don't fear it.

Don't run from it.

But treat it with lightness.

One wife I know brings her huffing and puffing husband to earth each time he sounds off by merely saying "Boo" to him.

That deflates his ego faster than arguments.

A Friendly-Making Trick to Use

One trick to rid yourself of an inferiority feeling, is to learn the trait of being friendly with people.

You are a little fellow, have no job of importance, no money—but you have a warm soul, a kind spirit, and people like to be around you for you inspire them. You can't offer them much knowledge or information, and you are no entertainer; but you have one quality: you are a good sounding board.

You get a lift when people talk to you. It overcomes your inferiorities. You beam and glow.

The other person becomes as friendly as you, and this makes you glow even more.

You then realize here is one trait where you are superior to others. It stimulates you to know this. It gives you courage; and one day you wake up with a whole flock of friends.

So try this trick. Make it Rule Three in overcoming a handicap: *Radiate Warmth and Friendliness To All.*

*

Learn to be superior in the art of friend-making.

Life's Ugly Ducklings

People who are ugly ducklings soon develop personalities to keep your eye away from their less attractive features.

Tall, gawky people can soon distinguish themselves in other ways to a point where their abnormal height is of no consequence. Flo Ziegfeld capitalized on tall chorus girls. A store in Dallas features garments for Tall Girls. For remember, tall people are as unfortunate as short ones. They have a different sort of problem in life, and a taller complex to overcome.

Many a famous enchantress in history was tall, yet had the shorter Caesars and Mark Antonys and Don Juans after them, clamoring at their door steps. Their height was no handicap, for they learned how to handle their height gracefully.

Sex Life of an Empress

"She isn't a beauty," say her friends, "but she sure has charm."

How often have you heard that of famous people? Eleanor Roosevelt, for example—or others who sold you charm instead of facial form.

Charm can be used to hide a handicap.

You can learn the tricks of charming people with your mannerisms; your conversation; your sincere feelings for others.

An Empress of Russia did just that, and it is reported reliably that her charm, not her looks, kept her in love well into her sixties! Without whole wheat germ!

Men wanted to be with her in preference to some glamorous, but stupid, lady in waiting. Her name: Catherine, Empress of Russia.

And from her we could easily get our Fourth Rule in diluting an inferiority complex: *Charm People Into Admiring You.*

Learn to Be Daring

Be daring.

Psychologists say that is another way to go places in life, by deflating a complex that is hounding you.

Steinmetz was daring enough to make mathematics and electronics his forte in life, and few ever noticed his deformity. They saw only a great brain in action.

Search yourself for some hidden gift God gave you. It may still be buried inside you. Maybe it is an ability to charm people by playing the piano, writing, singing, bowling, card playing or merely being friendly to others and in so doing, cultivate their respect and attention.

Avoid being a name dropper.

That's a sign, say the psychologists, of a "lowly birth."

Check grabbing is said to be a sign of early poverty trying to assert itself.

Only too often the richest man in town dresses in inexpensive clothes and drives an old car. He doesn't feel he must impress people with his importance through flashy clothes and cars. His bank statement does that for him; so he accepts his success graciously as you must always do when you reach the top of the ladder.

Remember, the higher up the ladder you go, the bigger a target you are for others to shoot at. And the more obvious you become to others—especially at your rear end.

Edison, Ford, Shakespeare Lacked Education

Beware of the back slappers in life.

They give you a big Texas-size hello, then slap you on the back—as they start talking about themselves.

Just like the cartoonist's idea of a Hollywood actor who enters a room and says, "Let's talk about something interesting—*myself*."

These are traits that keep you down in the doldrums. So they must be cast aside. You do this by first analyzing yourself to see if you have halitosis, mannerisms or carbuncles that are annoying others, and then eliminate them.

Also forget your lack of education.

Many successful people had little formal education, but developed lots of "brains." Edison, Ford, Shakespeare left school early. In fact, Edison never made the fourth grade and Ford got only to the sixth grade. But they made good, didn't they?

It is perhaps well they never did go to college—so they could hire college graduates!

The Story of Marilyn Monroe

Marilyn Monroe, the modern symbol of a love girl, lacked love as a child. She was hungry for parental love, it is said, for she had only an orphanage for a home.

Yet she overcame this handicap of birth, and became the great symbol of love; now men whistle as she wobbles by.

There are other such Horatio Alger stories of plowboys who became presidents and shoeshine boys who made fortunes.

These were fiction stories, but all around you are true life stories that often excel Horatio Alger's wildest dreams.

Would the late Hemmingway, asks psychologists, have

written better if he'd graduated from Harvard? Or Shaw if he was a college man? Or Shakespeare if he was head student of a college class?

The Story of Greta Garbo

A girl who had to earn her money in her teens by putting soap on men's beards in a barber shop became the famous Greta Garbo.

She went to the top, but once there, she didn't press her success. She retired from it to enjoy it all the better. To see her now you must watch a late, late TV program, but then you'll say, "She's still good."

An Irish girl named Kelly became Princess of Monaco, and a Baltimore divorcee named Wally Simpson made a king love her so much he gave up the crown for her.

Stories true in life, yet far more dramatic than book stuff.

Big opportunities lie ahead for you.

The day of making a million—or a million friends—is here right now.

Today, tomorrow—the next day.

Just set your own sights at your own target!

Your Success Is No Handicap

Being born with the golden spoon need not be a handicap, but often is. It wasn't, as I said, with Rockefeller and Ford—nor is it with a man named Kennedy whose famous political father and his wealth didn't hurt his progress. He became President of the United States, the highest honor.

Thomas Watson, Jr., of IBM fame, followed his dad successfully, and Averill Harriman, Governor of New York, overcame his golden spoon birth.

Herbert Hoover, Jr., and Robert Taft are other examples

of not being spoiled by the handicaps of wealth and famous parents . . . nor the Rothschilds.

Papa Rothschild had a handicap of a different sort. He was born in the ghetto, but Meyer Anschel Rothschild emerged to lead the world in finance.

He overcame the ghetto—his children overcame his wealth.

None of the family let their great wealth spoil their outlook. They made use of it.

The Skeleton-in-Closet Complex

One deterent to success is often some Uncle Ed in the family, whose antics of one sort or another, from too much drink to too much in the marriage line, often embarrasses sensitive members of the family and gives them complexes.

Uncle Ed gets them down, so the family gets a complex because of him. They fear he is ruining their social and business life, and they want to hide Uncle Ed in a dark closet with the skeletons.

On the other hand, psychologists will tell you that a brilliant member of the family can also give others a complex of another sort. They feel unlearned in his presence, and this hurts their pride and makes them feel inferior.

Outstanding workers in a factory can give other workers an inferiority complex. Cities can give other cities a complex.

You must over-ride such fears, and keep the complex away before it begins to eat your soul insidiously.

Dancing to His Tunes

As reported, skinny Arthur Murray always got a complex, as a boy, when others around him started to dance at school proms and elsewhere. This got Murray down. He went overboard on an inferiority complex, but look what happened when he pulled out!

He formed a chain of dancing schools, no less!

Can you imagine a boy who was laughed at for his dancing, teaching others how to dance?

Well, Arthur Murray did just that. He did something about his youthful lack of dancing ability.

Today you dance to his tunes! He calls the steps!

No Errol Flynn Here

People can form wrong images of people, and these people often get inferiority complexes.

Many a blonde actress has been termed "wow" girl, yet at heart she is not the "blondie" her name implies. Much better to be called a "brain girl," she thinks, than a "wow girl." One buxom actress began to study in school again, and started to "cultivate culture and brains."

People can and do get wrong images of you.

Did you know that the author of *Cat on a Hot Tin Roof* and *A Street Car Named Desire,* those worldly plays, was not an Errol Flynn in life—but was once a Caspar Milquetoast named Tennessee Williams?

His shyness with others was almost abnormal. Nearly morbid. Yet he asserted himself, and if you go to one of his movies you'll see a sign: ADULTS ONLY.

Many famous crooks are cowards at heart, such as Dillinger and Capone; and many a shy guy when faced with death becomes a hero.

What then is this fifth rule to overcome a complex?

It might well be: *Seek The Opposite Of What Others Think You Are.*

Might Be Worth Trying

You fear others will laugh at your dress, so you don't go to the party. People think you are stuffy. You are not. You show them—for you become the world's greatest party giver.

A new image then is born of you in minds of people.

You hate books—so become an athlete. You got kicked around as a child, so win the world's prize fighting championship. You change the image of yourself in the eyes of others who say, "I didn't think he had it in him." But you did.

This "turn about" method of overcoming a handicap complex, really works. The point being in these particular cases: don't follow what you hate in life, instead pursue what you like.

And once you've gained the goal, sell this image of yourself to others. Do this by living up to the image.

Men and Their Images

All of us leave images.

Toulouse-Lautrec, the little painter, a man of no sex appeal, did a "turn around" and became famous for can-can girl paintings. And he had love affairs. At least, that was the final image of the little fellow.

Don Juan, of course, left the image of being a great lover as did the more modern Errol Flynn—yet perhaps at heart they were once shy, wobbly, and unsure of themselves. In overcoming their backwardness toward the ladies each made that his strong point and big image.

Often love-making is a cover up for inborn shyness.

A man once sold the world he was a great surgeon. He left that image until he tired of it. Then he sold the world he was a famous world war pilot. Remember? And also he was a monk. He loved to leave such images behind him, and he perfected them and for years got away with his dupe until finally he was exposed. You read the exposure in *Life* magazine.

His picture, though wildly published, isn't hindering him

from once again manufacturing another image of himself to sell the world.

This impostor proves one thing: *you can be what you want!* But it behooves you to watch out what you want, for as I've said: *you'll get it!*

Your Moment of Truth

You saw how Juan Belmonte, man of weak legs, invented and started a whole new scheme of bull fighting by weaving the bull around him, not leaping from the bull. A Texas gal named Pat McCormick decided she'd do a man's job and fight bulls, and today is one of several women matadors.

When the urge comes to your soul, give it fertilization. Let it take hold and grow.

Face your own moments of truth.

Don't hide from them.

Bring them into the light.

And that might be our final and sixth rule in overcoming an inferiority complex: *Don't Hide The Weakness! Limelight It!*

For a complex, out in the open, can be observed and whipped. Hidden inside it will breed on and on, until some "couch doc" locates it for you and brings it into the light of reasoning.

So Face Your Complex

It is said that all of us are born with some sort of a complex; but if we use it properly, we can harness it and make it work for us as have these others I have mentioned—by the very perverseness in people to do the opposite of what they are.

Women have become famous lawyers.

Men have become famous clothing designers.

Women are running business; men are becoming cooks.

So face your complex full in the eye. Decide to whip it—or to make it work for you. Decide to do the opposite of what you believe you are, or capitalize on the complex and put it to work for you as did Arthur Murray and Elsa Maxwell.

Just have a goal. For this keeps you going.

Marlene Dietrich could not act in the early days—so she sold her leg appeal and became famous in the movie, *The Blue Angel.*

Many a Purple Heart has been given to a boy who, in his home town, was called shy and quiet by his friends and teachers.

Just remember: we have only one fear to fear and that's fear itself. You *can* become captain of your shy soul. Master of your bashful fate.

How?

By six Rules, and here they are again so you'll remember them all the rest of your lives:

Rule 1.   See Only The Good Things In Which You Excel.

2.   Play Up The Weakness If Need Be.

3.   Radiate Warmth And Friendliness To All.

4.   Charm People Into Admiring You.

5.   Seek The Opposite Of What Others Think You Are.

6.   Don't Hide The Weakness—Limelight It!

To Make Instant Friends
Through Proper Ways To Greet People
Try These Rules

Make the other fellow happy—happy to have met you.

Don't make him twice glad, glad to have met you—glad he is leaving you.

Avoid such hackneyed greetings as, "How are you?", "Please ta meecha!" or the disinterested, "Hello."

Also avoid such robust greetings as, "Put it there . . . !" You need not blow over a fellow with your greeting, nor do you need to be trite or bland.

Try to say something that will interest him, or raise his ego, such as, "Bill has often spoken of you," or, "I have often wanted to meet you."

There are many little personal greetings that will immediately sell yourself to others such as:

"Didn't I see you at the Jaycee dance?"

"Are you related to Mayor Green?"

Personalize as much as possible, and when you are not able to, then use such complimentary words as:

"It is a real pleasure to meet you."

"I am very happy to meet Helen's friends."

People form snap judgements of your greetings. So make this first impression a favorable one for you.

6

If you want people to do things for you
try these methods that date back
into Greek history

*"Every product of genius must
be a product of enthusiasm."*

One day in Athens I was talking with John Popadakis of
Olympic Airlines, friend of Mr. Emmanuel Frangopulos, the
great Greek ASTA travel agent who is up on worldly events.
We were discussing Greek dignity as it pertains to winning
goodwill and admiration.

I said to them: "You constantly point to the high arches
in the architecture and ask me to note some small detail. You
open a cupboard, a trunk, or some container and invite me to
observe hidden details. Tell me," I asked, "how many people
note such details?"

John hesitated a moment before he replied. "The workers
are aware of the hidden workmanship, and so is God."

I saw the lesson I was being given.

Greek workmanship lasts (as has the Acropolis) because it

75

has the heart of the workers in it as well as the master's hand.

"How does a person, in true Greek manner," I went on, "convince others to do such painstaking workmanship on places high above the observer's eye? What makes them want to do such fine work? What secret did the Greek discover centuries ago to encourage careful workmanship?"

I was thinking of our modern workers. How slip-shod many were. How little they cared for details, especially if hidden from the eye of the user. Nor did they care if what they made became suddenly obsolete in a few short years, or actually fell apart.

The answer I received was typical of Greek history.

Make People Part of the Act

That seemed to be the first rule to get cooperation of others. At once I saw the reason for the tactic: for people who are part of a performance perform best. They do a better job than people on the side-lines.

Statler, the famed hotel man, always would say, "Never tell an employee to do anything without taking him into your confidence and telling him why you want a thing done."

I can well remember how Statler practiced his own preaching. One day, in front of me, he asked a bell boy to go to a certain room and shut the window. Before the bell boy had a chance to grumble at such a menial job maids could do, Statler said, "There is an expensive rug by the window, and a rain storm is coming up. It may ruin the rug."

The bell boy then had a role to play—and he sprang into action to save a rug, not to close a window.

Remember the Greek rule: *to get willing and immediate support from people, make them part of the act. Explain the WHY behind the request.*

The Art of the Retreat

Our discussion that bright Greek morning in a side-walk cafe in Athens brought up another ancient method (as good today as in Socrates' time) in motivating people to your way of thinking. This method was to "back up a little before your charge, for in retreating you prompt people to move forward toward you."

I recently observed in London a good example of this "art of the retreat."

It concerned a Jaguar salesman, if he can be called that, since he was more of the diplomat than a salesman. He never once over-sold. He was inclined to stand aloof in front of a car, and through silence dramatize this king of cars much as one would with a Rubens' painting.

He was willing and able to discuss each point, but you had to prod him. He offered only the answer to your question. His method was to retreat to increase your interest.

The point is that when you have something of real value to offer others, it is better to under-sell the idea; for in pushing you often push the other person clear out of reach.

Be willing.

Be friendly.

But don't push so hard that others are forced to retreat themselves. Instead, lead them tactfully along your line of reasoning. Make them thirsty for what you have; this will win them faster.

For thirsty people are more willing.

And hungry people are more cooperative—more anxious.

I know one bean manufacturer who always insists on "thin men" to write his advertisements, saying, "They can appreciate my beans."

That may be far-fetched, but it has a point: hungry people are more responsive, as the Communists know only too well.

You can make people mentally hungry for what you have, or want them to do; make their mouths water in anticipation.

How to Give "Authority"

In Athens that day I learned another B. C. method of making willing people from reluctant ones.

It was to give AUTHORITY.

The army of every land knows this technique, which is why there are endless titles given from private, to corporal and up the line to generals with stars.

"How do you handle reluctant children?" I once asked Bob Blesh, of John J. Pershing School in Dallas which my daughter (not reluctant) attended at the time. "How do you take wild kids and make them good workers?"

"I give them titles," said Principal Blesh. "I recall one particularly recalcitrant boy. He was forever teasing the girls. He had his teasing down to an art. When one day I called him in, I asked him to be Chief Monitor, the Head Boy, and to keep the other children in line. The fellow's face brightened. He was to be an Indian Chief now, not a renegade. He became our best student."

A firm makes a "straw boss" out of an ordinary bench worker. "You are now in line," they'll tell him, "to be a foreman." He now has a reason to become a good worker and be on time. He's the last to rush off with the crowd at the day's end. He shows great interest in better workmanship, in true Grecian style.

Ask—Don't Order

We all like to be leaders.

Give us a title—or an assignment of importance—and we are bound to do our best job.

The garbage collector is now a SANITARY WORKER. The ticket seller is a Salesman. The milk man now sells "dairy products," not bottles of milk.

The man who lays rugs in your home or office is an Interior Decorator after a fashion. He has been given training in the business. He works better when you ask his opinions, and often he is successful in selling you a better rug—or an extra rug for another room. He is quick to point out the advantages of rubber padding underneath the new rug. His title makes him alert to such things.

So look about your business or home to see where you can give someone a title of importance, or at least an assignment of importance.

Tell your son he is now Head Bozo of the bedroom: "You are now in charge of keeping things in order with the other children."

Ask advice from the man who mows the lawn: "Tell me, since you are an expert on yard work, what would you suggest for over here?"

He will respond to such tact.

He will "advise" you; and when you work with him, you'll find he now has a personal interest in what he is doing for you.

Do the same with the plumber, the electrician, the TV repair man—the chap who adjusts your kitchen gadgets. Invite them to give you ideas, suggestions, advice. You'll be surprised what information you'll get, in addition to having a man now taking a sincere interest in your work and your problems.

All Presidents of the United States use this technique. They have to seek constant aid and advice from others, and when they ask for help, they gain immediate attention and action; the response is far greater than when they issue an order.

All governmental heads who are successful use this technique, and it is one to add to your own skills in getting others around you to respond favorably to your requests.

Ask—don't order!

World's Most Lonesome Word

The great persuaders of history use the word "we."

"We'd like to do this," they will say, then perhaps add, "What is your opinion of *our* doing it this way?"

When someone says, "I want this done this way," he will get it done if he is the boss, but it won't be done with alacrity. It will be done with grumbles and grunts, and that is no way to get people working for you.

"We'll be better off, don't you think, doing it this way?" invites the boss. The worker thinks a moment, gives his opinion. Both of them, together, do the job. The worker is part of the act, not a menial cog. It is "we" that gets things done.

This is good tact not only for governmental heads and business leaders—but also householders. Talk "we"—not "I." Make everyone a part of the "we" act.

Lincoln in his famous Gettysburg address used "we" constantly. Recite that address and note the many times he said "we" and not "I."

"*We* are met on a great battlefield . . . *we* have come to dedicate . . ."

That's the language that makes everyone a part of the great show!

Make it "we"—not "I."

"I" is a lonesome word!

A Trick of Great Leaders

People like to belong to groups.

That is why you see so many "organizations" these days.

People like to brag about being a member of some society, association, country club and so on. It gives them status.

It is a form of snob appeal to be a member of some outstanding group in town.

That is why firms organize "Foreman's Groups," why they have special picnics and shindigs for certain employees, making them feel good. Others are hungry to gain the status that will permit them to attend such affairs. The donkey and the carrot psychology again.

When a Commando Group is formed in the armed services, it becomes the envy of those not chosen. Only the best soldiers are invited. This then makes others struggle harder. Such groups respond faster and more willingly than the ordinary GI, for they are Commandos.

The Marine Corps, of which I am a reserve officer, did the same. As a procurement officer I made applicants sell ME on why they wanted to be a Marine. I never sold them. In fact, I made the Marine Corps sound tough.

Napoleon discovered this technique years ago. He'd call his army "Men of the Russian Campaign." He told them they were "hand picked" for a hard assignment. This inflated their ego. Made them fight harder. He said, "You may tell your families you were especially chosen for the invasion of Russia." He got extra vigor from his men with this technique of leadership.

So make others part of your show.

Give them a feeling of being wanted—of being important.

Then they will put their hearts into the assignment, as well as their brawn.

It's "We," Not "I"

YOU is the most important word in any language.

In fact, many languages have two types of the word "you."

One for general use, plus a familiar "you" for close friends and the family.

"YOU and I can do this," says the leader. The other's ego inflates and together they put shoulder to shoulder and push on.

The person who hears "we" doesn't feel like a paid worker, but a member of the team.

Knute Rockne always said "we." He invited "team work," not stardom in any one player.

Cooperation is a great way to get people to work.

In conclusion, put to use the formula of the Greeks. Get fine workmanship, enthusiasm, and cooperation through these tactics:

1. Make people part of the act.

2. Retreat a little before your charge.

3. Make 'em hungry and thirsty.

4. Let people be Indian Chiefs.

5. Give titles wherever possible.

6. Use the word "we" and "you" constantly.

7. Keep the lonesome "I" out of your conversation.

"Compliments give the other person STATURE."

Four Tested Ways
To Handle Complaints And Maintain
Goodwill And Friendships

The art of leading one who complains to your way of thinking can be summed up in four steps:

Step 1: **HEAR HIM OUT.** He expects you to listen to every word, and in doing so you let him blow off dangerous steam. Soon he runs down. His anger dissipates and he relaxes to see what you now have to say.

Step 2: **REPEAT HIS COMPLAINT.** Fool him. Don't alibi or ridicule. But instead repeat his complaint (without sarcasm) to let him know you fully realize his gripe. In hearing his own complaint from another, it often doesn't sound so good to him. He is inclined to minimize it.

Step 3: **CORNER THE COMPLAINT.** Give in to his minor kicks by either side-stepping them or acknowledging them on the spot. *But get behind his one major complaint.* Then solve it and shake hands. You've won him.

Step 4: **SAVE A FRIEND—NOT YOUR FACE.** Never treat a complaint lightly. Take it seriously. Avoid giving excuses and alibis. Save the friend, not your face.

7

How to make your daydreams come true
and at the same time bring your
castles in the air down to solid earth

"No one knows what he can do till he tries."

There are many kinds of dreams in a man's life: but usually two predominate.

They are Nightmares and Daydreams.

The Nightmares we can pass up. They are fragments of the day's bad thoughts and events; dreams brought only worry or the Lobster Newburg at dinner.

Daydreams are another thing: they are man's hopes in life. His desires, ambitions—his goal, his target.

He follows his daydreams as a dog follows his master.

Many of the world's famous people had humble daydreams that became magnificent actualities: first as children sitting with a fishing pole; then in schoolrooms gazing out windows; then in places of business—daydreams of adventure, romance, wealth and fame.

Charlie Schwab became president of a great steel firm by first daydreaming, then setting his sights on the target.

Charlie E. Wilson as a $7.00 a week employee feared poverty but his daydreams were so vivid that he became president of General Electric Company. Wanamaker built his stores from daydreams that included doing away with the common policy of *caveat emptor,* let the buyer beware. A former president of the Illinois Central Railroad as a youngster swept station platforms, daydreamed of going up the railroad's ladder of success, and he did.

Daydreams get you places in life.

*

What are daydreams?

They are dreams we usually have in daylight, rather than during the night. They can be controlled whereas night dreams cannot. They are called daydreams because people get that longing look in their eye as they stare skyward, dreaming about themselves as a Knight in armor or a King or Queen of big business. It is their hopes coming to the surface; their desires and ambitions seething within them restlessly. The daydreams are usually interrupted when someone says, "A penny for your thoughts."

Any One Can Daydream

Daydreams built fortunes.

Hilton daydreamed about owning the Waldorf Astoria Hotel. It came true.

Columbus daydreamed . . . so did Magellan . . . and Salk and the big man in your own home town.

Can anyone have daydreams?

Or is the day of daydreaming over, along with adventure, romance and new worlds to conquer? Aren't all worlds conquered today? No—opportunities still exist.

Today anyone can daydream, and still go places. We just had a navy man daydream of flying through space. Shepard did just that. We now have men daydreaming of going to the moon, and they will. Others are more earthbound and are daydreaming of owning their own home, being a leader among men, having a bigger car, going on world trips. They will. Indeed, daydreams never lose their popularity. Adam started daydreaming years ago, and his descendants will continue to daydream of yet-to-be imagined wonders.

The Story of a Bullfighter

Death in the bull ring some afternoon frightened Juan Belmonte.

Unlike El Gallo and other matadors before him, Juan's legs were weak and not nimble enough to leap away from 2,000 pounds of charging bull, but he daydreamed of a new technique: that of making the bull pass in front of his wobbly legs. He started a new era of bull fighting, one of using the muleta to wave bulls away and past the matador. It is now the accepted method of bullfighting. Matadors who now leap away get booed.

Juan and his "frozen legs" became a symbol of good bullfighting. Others caught on to the art and became perhaps more spectacular in the feat, such as the famed Manolete, but all had to follow the principles that Belmonte's daydreams conceived.

If a shy Belmonte can bring his daydreams to life, so can you.

And here is how:

It is a formula I found after interviewing nearly 1,000 men and women whom I wrote up in a column called "Success Secrets" for George Little, head of General Features Syndicate. George had told me:

"Why don't you ask the 1,000 successes you have written about how they became a success? Many are millionaires today . . . if not in actual gold of the realm, at least spiritually. There may be a hidden pattern, a definite formula that runs through the successful lives of these 1,000 people."

I liked publisher Little's idea, and started a program of asking my 1,000 "rich people" what plan they followed. Did they have a formula, a rule, a certain series of steps they followed to success? Strangely, when I analyzed all the replies, I did see a similarity, a pattern that followed each person's steps to success, and I give it to you as follows:

Six Steps to Success

1. *Know What You Want in Life.*

   If you don't know what you want, how can you get it?

   You must have a daydream: a goal, a target in life. A castle in Spain that needs building. Gather your ideas from others, from reading and by inner desires. See the image of what you'd like in life: to be a king, a leader, a business tycoon, a happily married man or woman—to be a lawyer, doctor, school teacher, an inventor, banker, or writer? Let your wildest hopes come to the surface. They may seem wild at the moment, but never fear, what today seems impossible becomes possible later on. Just dream about what you want in life. Set the target. Each of my 1,000 rich people had daydreams, castles in Spain, to start with.

2. *Put the Daydream on Paper.*

   This is important for it makes sure the daydream doesn't disappear. It can, you know. But once it is blueprinted on paper, it remains your challenge forever. The Empire State Building itself was once only a daydream, just as tomorrow's moon-ships are. For in getting things on paper, my "millionaires" claimed the daydream suddenly materialized. It came into sight, out of the mind's eye onto paper. You now have something concrete to see with your eyes. So put your daydream on paper. Look at it in the daylight. You may want to alter the daydream and castle as it is being built, but you now have a visual plan to follow, just like an architect.

3.   *Know Where to Start.*

At first you may have your cart before the horse. That's all right. You'll see the error and correct it; and soon you'll find through trial and error where to start the daydream in earnest. Painters go to Paris. Singers to Milan. Bankers to Wall Street. Oil men to Texas. Diplomats to Washington. For in the proper locale everybody is talking the same thing. To talk oil in Boston is out of character; to talk designing in Anchorage is off-beat. Stick to the proper reservation for then others can help bolster your daydream for they'll speak your language. There people live, eat and sleep with similar hopes and ambitions. Tomatoes don't grow best in mountain lands, but coffee does. Daydreams grow faster in the proper "soil." So pick your best locale to start to cultivate your daydream.

4.   *Set it in Motion.*

You've found your life's ambition. It is blue-printed—have the courage to paste it on your bathroom mirror as a daily reminder—and set yourself up in the proper atmosphere to make your daydream mushroom and take seed. Now you must take Step 4, and that is: *set your daydream in motion.* There are close to three million inventors' daydreams filed in Washington, most of which are not seeding but going to seed because no one is keeping them in motion. Don't let this happen to your daydream. Start it off, humbly perhaps at first, but at least get it off the ground. Then as it catches fire, keep it in motion. A hoop keeps going by little urges of the boy's stick, but only after the hoop is in motion. Momentum also keeps daydreams going as it does hoops, trains and motors. Fortunes cannot be made if the daydream lies dormant or stagnant. The bum sits on the park bench with a mind filled with daydreams that are motionless. He will tell you, "If wishes were horses us beggars would ride." Bullets never kill until they are shot from the gun—and daydreams never mature until they are shot from the brain. Once they take flight, their success is within your reach.

5.   *Don't Settle for Less.*

My 1,000 millionaires had another thing in common: they

didn't settle for less than the full daydream. They kept their daydream going through many setbacks, many false starts—but they wouldn't accept a castle in Spain only half built. It was whole hog or none. No one stopped building the Empire State Building at the thirtieth floor saying, "Well, we should be glad we got it up this far." That thinking kills the daydream. If you dream about a Jaguar car, don't settle for a Fiat.

If your goal is a mink coat, don't settle for rabbit. If your daydream includes making a million dollars, don't settle for one cent less—don't weaken yourself. Your determination will falter. You'll wake up with nothing. Go clear to the pinnacle. Then proceed to another daydream to top this one, and reach the next pinnacle. Get lazy half way, and the daydream will crumble and you'll see your castle in ruins at your feet.

6. *Know When to Relax.*
Dont's settle for less—but don't be greedy.

Once you've gained your present goal, relax. At least temporarily. Get your breath as you enjoy seeing your dream come true. Sit back and reflect and restore your energy. The greedy one who pushes on endlessly and needlessly, never enjoys the fruits of his efforts. These people end up rich, but in the graveyard, and then some heir has the fun spending the fortune. My millionaires all knew the pitfall of over-pressure, each remembering that what he is today was his daydream ten years ago. Today's success is what he daydreamed about only a few years back. So don't settle for less—*but don't be overly greedy.*

This, therefore, is the six point formula to success through making your daydreams come true. Watch your castle in Spain rise before your eyes.

Follow this practical plan discovered by 1,000 successful men and women, and you, too, will be richer in life. You just can't miss.

Chapter Thought
Stand still and silently watch the world go by—and it will!

8 TESTED WAYS TO SELL YOURSELF TO OTHERS

Wheelerisms for success.

1. Pat others on the back before you kick them in the pants.
2. Take the blame.
3. Don't gossip, because others will worry about what you say of them in *their* absence.
4. When you leave people, leave only once. Many a friendship is broken at the door that you kept open too long.
5. Leave 'em laughing.
6. Let the other person monopolize the conversation, for you never learn when your own mouth is open.
7. Learn the art of "proper timing." Never phone others during a TV program. Phone them during "commercials."
8. Don't look bored. Rather, look alive and interested.

8

Beware of pseudo-admirers
or back-patters
and don't be one yourself
if you want to go places smoothly

> *"He who praises everybody praises nobody."*
> —Dr. Samuel Johnson in Boswell's *Life of Johnson*

It has been said by philosophers of old, "Fear your admirers for they discolor your perspective."

Actors especially, according to actress Jessica Tandy, must beware of false admirers, those back patters who have ulterior motives in their acclamations.

Too often a person has been spoiled by listening to adulation to the point where judgement is lost in the false-praise of the admirer. You then lose balance in life, and fail to go places smoothly.

Often, well-meant compliments from friends and family are taken too seriously by the recipient, and this upsets that person's good sense.

Jessica Tandy quotes this paragraph from *My Life in Art* by Stanislavski:

"Young actors, fear your admirers. Learn in time, from your first steps, to hear, understand and love the truth about yourselves. Find out who can tell you the truth and talk of your art only with those who will tell you the truth."

This advice to actors applies to bookkeepers, bankers, housewives, husbands, school children—to us all—for anyone of us can have our judgement colored by admiration, set off balance by too much praise. Too often do we become inflated by the false remarks of others designed to flatter our ego, regardless of truth.

The Rule to Use

The best guard against being thrown off balance by friends and others is this rule: *learn to evaluate your friends so you know which will honestly tell you the truth about yourself, whether the truth compliments or hurts our ego.*

Fear, as death itself, people with motives who falsely compliment you to throw you off your balance for their personal gain.

And when the time comes for you to praise—or criticize—others, do so honestly yourself.

There is no substitute for honesty.

To be sure, "Be friendly not frank" on most casual occasions with others, but when the times comes for frankness, be frank. But tell the truth as softly as you can. Put it in language that won't hurt or maim the other person. Don't kill incentive. Be gentle with your criticsm.

How much better to say: "When I was your age, Jim, I was a terrible bookkeeper. I'm still no good. But I did learn this way of doing the job better."

That erases the sting of blunt criticisms. It dulls the criticism. It makes you a normal error-prone person yourself, not a Tin God; and the one being corrected will accept the criticism easier than if you were to blurt out:

"Jim, you fool. You're stupid. Any idiot in his right mind would know better than to do the job that way. Not let ME show you how it should b done!"

That kills Jim's incentive.

It injures his pride.

His self-respect dwindles.

He becomes a resentful person and you become friendless. You may suddenly find an enemy on your hands. Not a physical one; but a more insidious mental enemy.

Compliment and Then Criticize

Another tactic in the art of gentle criticism is to compliment before you criticize.

Say: "Jim, I liked the way you did that job for the Smith firm. It was a great piece of work. But what happened to the Brown assignment. Something go wrong?"

This allows Jim a chance to puff up over one job well done, and save some face on the other.

It is an effective but friendly technique.

It will help you to reach the upper rung on the ladder of success. Any executive, any trainer, any teacher or any parent will gain more respect for himself if he learns the art of first complimenting, then criticizing. It is a method that will carry you forward in the social world.

Plan to find something on which to glorify the person you plan to criticize or correct; then offer the suggested ways of doing the assignment the way you feel is the right way.

Any good movie director knows this. He will always compliment first. "Bravo, bravo on that bit about the mistress, but pul-eeze, less arm emoting on the love scene. More with the face—less with the arms. Get it?"

Sure the actress gets it. She has been fed syrup first, and can now take the bitter stuff.

Be a talented director yourself.

Learn to feed others the things that make them feel proud before you deflate them. People who have just been complimented can take a lot of correction.

Always be quick to let the other person save face by telling you why he did something. In many cases when he explains, he will discover by himself the error of his ways and be quick to give himself self-criticism, thereby saving your face. And in many cases, when he explains his reason, you might find his way the better one after all.

It is best to say, "Tell me, Jim, why was it done this way?"

This gives Jim a chance to explain. From his explanation you can then decide whether or not Jim was right.

The Hong Kong Story

Lincoln once said:

"If you would win a man to your cause, you must first convince him that you are his sincere friend."

One way is never to rear up and shout, "Your best friend won't tell you how stupid you are, but I will!"

That's not a good way to start off correcting others.

One evening I sat relaxed in the Marco Polo Restaurant in Hong Kong, adjacent to the Peninsula Hotel. I was talking with the proprietors, Mr. and Mrs. Emile Soutter, and the subject got around to Marco Polo himself. Mr. Soutter said to me:

"There was a great salesman. He knew the art of making friends of strangers. He came to China years ago and made friends first before he started to negotiate for the wares he was to take back to Italy.

"Marco Polo liked to mix with strangers. He acquired this

trait back home in Venice, so that when he visited a new land he instinctively started making friends. His father, Nicolo, and his uncle, Maffeo, noted the friendly nature of Marco, and took him on one of their trips to the Orient.

"China was a land of riches, but no one could go there and rob them. You had to win over Kublai Khan before he permitted you to take his wares even for a good price.

"It took six years to make the trip from Venice to China. In this time Marco Polo was briefed by his dad and uncle. 'Be friendly,' they said, 'be honest with all you meet. Avoid false compliments. Never admire dishonesty.' And Marco did well, and I guess that is why we named this the Marco Polo Restaurant."

So spoke Emile Soutter.

He Wins Kublai Khan

Instead of trying to sway Kublai Khan to European ways of thinking, Marco Polo convinced Kublai Khan he wanted to learn about life in China. He spent months learning about China, and in so doing he won respect—and riches to take back home.

He learned the knack of making Kublai Khan thirsty and hungry to do business with his sincere visitor to China. This is a knack all must learn who want to win others to their cause.

First become a friend by getting the other person to do most of the talking. Be sincere while listening. Excite the other person's interest in telling you about *himself, his* life, *his* business—*his* hopes, ambitions and daydreams. Let him build *his* castle in Spain before your admiring eyes. This makes for real friendship.

After which you can do business with that person.

You have won a friend. A lasting one. You are ready now to present your case.

A Real Tel Aviv Seller

Most salesmen today know the art of first admiring something about a person's life, his surroundings, his family. He excites that other person to talk about himself, to let loose, relax, and get into a mood to be sold.

Across the street from the Dan Hotel in Tel Aviv, is a tiny jewelry shop. One day in the shop a wife of one of the owners approached Mrs. Wheeler. "That is an unusual star pin you are wearing. It is made of the best rose cut diamonds. Where did you find it?"

It took Mrs. Wheeler 15 minutes to tell the story of how she found it in a shop in Jerusalem. The woman listened with great interest, and after Mrs. Wheeler ran out of talk, the woman reached into some tissue paper and produced a companion piece of jewelry, saying, "This ring almost weeps to be with the pin you are wearing, it goes so well."

That's what I mean about selling!

*

Make 'em like you.
Listen well.
Compliment sincerely.
You'll go far in life if you do.

CHAPTER THOUGHT

When you must admire, do so sincerely. When you compliment, make it honest. For in so doing you open the way for your own suggestions.

A Big Secret To Avoid The Loss Of Goodwill And Business Profits

It is called by some the Socratic Method of getting others to say yes, yes, yes . . . before you bring up subjects to which they may answer no, nein, nyet.

The tactic is to start a conversation on points of agreement, even by saying, "We did agree last time that you would never go to Florida, right?" The other's head shakes that yes you are right, and you are both in agreement.

Then you proceed to get a few more similar Socratic "yeses," and then with the other's head in good momentum, you switch to a question that the other person may not have agreed with previously, but because he is now in a nodding and friendly mood, he may continue to nod in your favor.

Diplomats have developed this knack to a fine art. "My opponent last time said we are asking for too much money, is that not right?" To which all nod in approval. Perhaps he then says, "I agree that it did look like a big expenditure for so little, but then if the little were bigger, the expenditure would be worthwhile, am I not right?" And chances are he is right.

Faces are saved. Friends are made.

"No turned HIND-END-TO becomes on!"

9

If you want to win friends and friendships
try this simple two-word system
that top men in business
have proved works miracles

"The business of life is to go forward."

"Somebody cared!"

That was the two-word system I first heard of from Bob Newcomb when I asked him how, with American labor so belabored about poor quality, his firm was still able to creep to the top quality spot in short order and go head and shoulders over long established competitors.

"You entered the tape recording business late," I said to him in his neat Hollywood plant, "yet within two model series you have become the envy of other tape recorder manufacturers and the daydream of all recording enthusiasts. What's your system?"

It was then that Newcomb told me: "Somebody cared!"

"Cared? What do you mean?"

"I was the one who cared," he went on. "I wanted a perfect instrument. One that did not compromise with quality, one that met the tape users' needs. I made a mock-up of my idea of a recorder, one that could handle up to a ten and a half

101

inch spool that only professional models can accommodate. I then sent my hand-made instrument to a few enthusiasts to use and to criticize. They did. They saw I really cared about their needs, and they came back with innumerable practical suggestions.

"These field tests guided me in making a recorder that met the customer's needs and overcame criticisms of the present sets on the market. I then rebuilt my set ———— my castle in Spain as you'd call it, my daydream. I then sent a few sets to dealers to test out, hesitatingly I must admit, for my reputation lay in school room audio equipment which I make and sell. But the dealers acclaimed my set, and offered more suggestions for improvements which I made. A few sets were placed on the market for the public to buy. All approved of my living daydream, but asked if I could keep up the same custom, hand-made quality on a production line basis.

"I went to my workers. I told them I wanted to make quality sets. Would they help? They said they would. And they did. They now watch each screw, each wire—they put their hearts as well as their skilled fingers into backing me up with quality. In fact, each worker is his own quality supervisor, for each realizes that somebody cares for their skilled workmanship."

Indeed Bob Newcomb's "I care" system has paid off. I know. I bought a set long before I had known Newcomb, and when I saw his quality hand-made product, I wanted to meet the man. So do his dealers and customers at all music conventions he attends standing constantly by his machine, a man proud of having cared.

The Story of Walt

My dislike for poor workmanship drove me into buying an imported car. Then my troubles began. I could find no mechanic with an "I care" attitude to service it, until one day I found the man known as "Walt" at the Clarence Talley firm in Dallas. I saw his "I care" manner of covering the fender with a cloth before he worked over it. I saw his tool kit—a show room of instruments to fit everything on my car. I would watch him work with a patience that made me nervous, for when he'd try to silence a noisy door, he'd test it over and over and then insist on a bumpy drive for further testing.

Walt was fired from a firm after he had injured his back. Whenever he tried for a job, he was turned down by the insurance firm of that company because he was honest enough to admit his back injury. One day John Talley, who supervises the auto company's service department for his brother Clarence, gambled on Walt's employability because "the man was honest enough not to hide his back injury."

Walt cared about his reputation. John cared about Walt. And they have my business, for they care about Elmer.

He Makes Luggage

Again I saw this same "somebody cared" system operate when I purchased some Koch Fiberglass luggage. I saw how it defied "baggage smashers" around airlines, buses, trains and hotels. I admired the way it was made. I saw that somebody cared, and I looked up that man. He was the owner Koch, himself, who told me, "I cared about my customers. I cared about my reputation as a luggage maker. I told my workers I cared. They saw I cared, and they began to care, too, about their work. Result: we have a luggage that lasts. Unfortunately we can't sell to the same person each year, for our luggage lasts. But we are happy people."

And so is traveler Elmer happy!

The Minox Story

I saw the same "I care" attitude in the Minox camera, that little 3½ ounce one you wear on your belt for ready service when traveling. I spoke to Mr. G. Sause one day at his Minox plant outside of Frankfurt, Germany. I watched his careful method of making cameras, and how his men took pride in their work knowing that Herr Sause cared. He told me he had a proud reputation to maintain, and only careful workmanship on each and every one of the 200 parts in the camera would maintain that reputation. I later met his right-arm in America, Don Thayer, and saw how he cared, too.

That is why this little camera is the leader in the pocket-size field.

For when people know you care—they respond.

How to Have Friends

Let me say because of such care, I seldom need work on my Jaguar, on my Newcomb, on my Minox. They are all made to last, not to become shoddy through lack of care in workmanship.

When dad and mom care, son and daughter do better work around the house.

So the moral is: show the others around you that you care, and they will respond and care, too.

When "somebody cares," you find good workmanship and friendliness.

If you want to be a leader in your community, let it know you sincerely care.

It's a great technique among the true leaders of industry, one you can apply in your own home, service club, PTA group, or neighborhood.

People who care have lasting friends.

The Westinghouse Experiment

One day the Hawthorn plant of Westinghouse decided to make a test. They increased the lighting in the plant. Work improved. Quality went up. The head men then decided to see if it was possible to further improve quality by further stepping up the lighting. It was.

Then someone had another idea. He had the wattage of the lights *reduced,* when strangely quality again went up.

Perplexed, the bosses were at a loss. They couldn't understand how such things could continue to happen, for they assumed it was better lighting and ability to see easier that improved quality. Yet with reduced lighting, quality still rose.

One day an alert supervisor with an "I care" attitude discovered why production improved whether lighting was high or low. His finding proved one thing—that the workers realized "somebody cared about them," and they responded each time regardless of the specific intensity of the light.

An Insurance Firm Cares

The Hartford Life Insurance Company cared about the frequency of children being burned by fire. Youngsters often would not heed the usual parental warnings, or those of their school teachers. One day the firm issued Fire Chief Hats to a group of children.

"Here," said the parent or teacher, "be a Fire Chief and help watch out for fires!"

The kids got a kick out of playing Fire Chief. They saw their parents and teachers cared about their safety by instructing them dramatically about the dangers of fire. The places where this program was started showed a marked drop in incidents involving children and fire.

An insurance firm cared—and acted.

*

CARE, the packages that go around the world, win friends for us, for those receiving the packages say, "Americans care about ME!"

*

You will always win over others if you show you care.

A phone call to a dealer shows you care about his profits.

A call to a sick friend, shows you care. Sending letters and cards to people show you care.

The successful leaders in your community are people who show they care.

Fui Shui is the word for "neighborly friendliness" that motivates oriental city governments in their decisions about some civic change. If they plan a new street, they ask the neighborhood if it will make them happy. If not, the street is abandoned until the people of that neighborhood, who must live near the new street, will approve.

This "I care" attitude builds civic pride.

When a city council arbitrarily decides to relocate a street in the name of "progress," tears up a neighborhood, or does away with a park despite the objections of people, that council is short-lived at voting time for not caring.

Show That Somebody Cares

If you want to make friends, show an interest in them.

If they take a trip, phone to see how the trip went. If they are ill, inquire about them. If they are mentioned in the newspaper, phone and tell them you saw it.

Show interest in people around you. Let them feel "somebody cares" what they do.

Be careful about your CARE packages.

The Ron Fletcher Story

Ron Fletcher took an interest in the sick.

He noticed how their hospital beds could be raised or lowered at either end to make them more comfortable, yet when they returned to their homes for recuperation, their regular beds were less adaptable.

So Fletcher invented a bed that raised and lowered at either end simply by pushing a trigger. He "cared."

Today, in Dallas, Texas, he is the unseen friend of many a person who knows about Fletcher's caring for their comfort. Even those not ill use it to prop themselves up nights, to read or watch television in greater comfort.

By showing an interest in people, Fletcher today has a "care-full" business of caring for the needs (and pleasures) of people. And he has proved that fortunes can still be made if you care.

You, too, can make many friends—and profits—by taking an interest in people: their golf, their parties, their picnics, their troubles. You may not be a personal friend, but you can still show an interest. . . .

. . . by being a person who honestly cares!

CHAPTER THOUGHT

One tested and sure way to win others over, especially workers, is to show you care—the two-worded formula for success. When you care—so will others.

"I do not greatly care whether I have been right or wrong on any point, but I care a good deal about knowing which of the two I have been."—Samuel Butler

Your Check List To Get Things Done Faster In Life—Yet Not Tire You Out

Tom Kenny of *Dun's Review of Modern Industry,* feels that a person who has the art of getting things done quickly and easily goes places faster in life and is less tired out at the day's end. His advice list includes:

1. Avoid late starts. (The early bird gets the best worms).
2. Don't neglect people who may be open for business before 8:30.
3. Don't waste time with friendly folks who merely bolster your ego—but can't be of much help otherwise.
4. Avoid too large an area you can't get around to properly.
5. Avoid making excessive trips back to the office (or home).
6. Don't waste time visiting people when phone calls would do.
7. Don't burn energy by constantly "going back" to the same prospects.
8. Don't make an overly-detailed report on all you do.
9. Avoid poor routing of your daily calls and chores.
10. Don't fail to make appointments—and so avoid wasting valuable time in waiting rooms.

"The Emperor is rich but can't buy one extra year."

"3 early risings make an extra day."

10

When you do excel in something,
don't make the error of
hiding yourself behind
a mask of put-on modesty

"To be heard afar . . . bang your gong on a hill top"

There is a difference between bragging and being overly-modest, retiring and bashfully shy.

No one like a braggart. But we must admit the braggart isn't a shy one in a dark corner of life waiting for opportunity to come his way. The braggart is often offensive, and at times loud, annoying and a bore. Yet he is a person going places in life, but the hard way. Casanova, Don Juan, Hitler —all were braggarts, but were not buried in history.

The ideal person would be a modest fellow with the *push* of the braggart.

A person who is a leader—but tells the world about it in a soft spoken way, free of boasting, is a person much in demand.

Let's face it: if your qualities are hidden under a bushel, you will delay your arrival on top of the success ladder.

Neon lights were made to call attention, for the best-looking merchandise won't sell by itself, nor the prettiest dotted line sign itself. People can't get places in life without advertising their qualities and the features in which they excel.

The trick in "pushing yourself" is to do so firmly, but with low pressure advertising of your personal qualities.

You can't hang a sign around your neck saying, "I'm great!" You will only be ridiculed. But if you sit modestly in the corner, fail to engage in conversation, would rather stay home glued to TV than to be at an office party—your chances of rising to the top of the world's dust pile are very remote.

You must learn how to advertise yourself tactfully.

Progressive Charlie does it by contacts. He is forever at lodge meetings and service club luncheons and dinners and social gatherings of all kinds. He is always on some local committee. His name is constantly appearing—but it is not shouting, "Look at me do somersaults, boys!"

Indeed, it is tactful advertising of your wares through word of mouth by others that does the job for you.

Take It Easy!

One person wears a sandwich board that shouts EAT AT JOE'S. That's obvious advertising, like a kid going by on a bicycle and shouting, "Look, mom, no hands!" The billboard is good for commercial advertising, not for social.

You can accomplish the same advertising aim, silently and tactfully, by being seen at proper places: the Bankers' Club, the Sales Club, the Engineers' Club, the Insurance Club—fields in which you are interested in being part of the picture. The Foremen's Club does the same thing for the factory worker, just as the Friday Night Bowling Club does for the bench workers on the way up.

Be seen.

That's trick one in the art of self-exposure.

*

Some people advertise their wares through amusing or interesting and unusual traits of character or personality.

I appeared once on Groucho Marx's program. Here is a character with amusing antics that sells himself to others. He can get laughs through ridicule. His brother, Harpo, does it with a harp—and no words.

Imagine an entertainer not using words!

Charlie McCarthy gained fame—and he's a wooden image.

Your "line" in life can often be your best advertising feature. People often say, "When Joe arrives, boy, will the party begin!" Joe has created an image of himself as a hearty fellow, well met, a great joker whom everyone calls the "life of the party." That's his trade mark to make sure he isn't lost in a sea of faces.

Art Linkletter isn't funny—but he had a program, "People Are Funny," which identified him with funny events in people's lives. He rose above the great mass of humanity looking for jobs when his producer, John Guedel, took a piece of wrapping paper and wrote on it, "PEOPLE ARE FUNNY," signed his name and address and sent it to an advertising agency that had just lost a good account; Guedel then sold them the Linkletter program . . . and soon after the Groucho program.

Guedel knows it doesn't pay to hide in a dark corner.

The best ideas in your brain are of no commercial value until they are revealed to the world, preferably in a spectacular manner to attract attention.

But to be exotic with no purpose other than to attract attention is unworthy. You must have a definite purpose behind doing the unusual to gain attention. Jimmy Moran sold a refrigerator to the Eskimos to attract attention for his publicity firm. He once sat on an ostrich egg to hatch it, and he looked for he proverbial needle in a haystack—all attention getters, but all designed to show the world that he had ideas to sell.

Fit the Part!

Some people attract attention with bow neckties; others with high fashion clothing, as often observed on some actor or actress; some such as writers and newspaper correspondents, wear beards. The trick is not to be exotic just for the sake of attracting attention, but to sell some ability that is being lost through lack of sizzlemanship and dramatic flair.

The banker dresses in Brooks Brothers style clothing; but the beatnik wears loose sweaters, each trying in his way to sell his image to the world.

Tip: *When you dress to attract attention, be sure to fit your style of dress to your position in life.*

Look the part you play in life, or want to play.

The sports shirt is fine for the man who golfs at his country club; the striped formal trousers fit the diplomatic meeting in Washington.

That's the trick: *look the part you play in life.*

Few lawyers can wear country clothing to put over an image that they are just plain lawyers, unslick in city ways. Few juries fall for that trick today, although at one time it was the thing to look the part of the rube lawyer defending his poor client against the citified lawyer of the Big Corporation.

Look appropriately dressed for your work, whether it be the white uniform of a dentist, or clean overalls for a car mechanic. Look efficient; look the part.

The Maynard Brothers of Webcor, Harmon, Karmon, and Lansing speaker fame in the hi-fi world, look like they know their business. They seem actually to radiate information in their every action, mannerism and conversation. They have a trick of getting conversation around to their best point—that is, their great knowledge of hi-fi. Then they advertise their wares tactfully.

Yet brother Harold is deaf in one ear. "My tin ear," he tells people, "but my other ear is tuned to good music. Here, listen to this new Webcor sound off."

Both Maynards, John and Harold, are leaders in their field in the Southwest.

*

You must sell an image of yourself to others.

Ability is often taken for granted. That is wrong. Latent ability is useless to the owner. Bullets in guns are no good until they fly at their targets. The same goes for ability. Letting it lie unseen and unsung is no way to sell yourself to others.

A survey showed that in the banking field 77% of men with ability failed to get ahead in life because they neglected to get the attention of the proper officials.

Their ability was lost in the shuffle.

It is fine to be humble—but don't over-do it if you want to go places.

Be quick to say, *"I can handle that assignment!"*

Tell people, *"That's down my line."*

Then set out to prove it.

Be just as quick to tell others, *"That's not for me—but this is!"*

You'll gain respect by not being a Jack-of-All-Trades—a Know-it-All. Be fast to admit a failing—quick to highlight your strong points.

Highlight Yourself!

Your superiors don't have x-ray eyes, nor microscopes to examine your worth. You must call it to their attention in a nice manner. So be alert to highlighting your talents, fast to call attention to whatever you do well. It is not necessary to stand on your hands in front of a Hollywood studio to let some producer know you are there; nor is it proper to carry a sandwich board around at office parties; but neither is it wise to hide in a corner and hope-to-gosh somebody will discover you.

Be humble. Don't flaunt yourself. Be shrewd about ways to bring yourself to the attention of others with a soft-sell manner, not with hi-pressure brash. The lad had the right idea when, seeing the long line of office boys applying for a job, he sent a note in ahead of him saying, "Don't hire anyone until you see the red-headed boy at the end of the line."

He wasn't taking the chance of not being interviewed.

Charles Markham, later president of the Illinois Central Railroad, always swept his platform particularly well as a young sweeper when the train went by carrying his superiors. One day a top brass noted the industrious youth sweeping every corner of the platform with gusto and care. Charlie was seen—and soon promoted. He kept on "being seen" and being promoted until he was made president of the railroad.

Yul Brynner attracts attention to his great acting ability in another way: he has shaved his head bare!

The trick to gain attention of others is to use showmanship —but not be just a show off!

*

IBM attracted attention to its machines with one word: THINK. You find the motto in business offices everywhere, offices that would never display an advertising sign that read: BUY AN IBM MACHINE. Yet this one word THINK was good advertising.

Teddy Roosevelt attracted attention with his Big Stick technique and the one word, "Dee-lighted"; FDR by a long cigarette holder, and President Kennedy with his lovely wife, saying, "I'm the husband."

Will Rogers did it in many ways, one of which was to make such quotable statements as "I never met a man I didn't like," and another chewing gum. Rube Goldberg used the opposite approach and said, "I meet many men I don't like." You see he was a political cartoonist deflating the images of famous people in public life.

Frank Buck attracted attention with a pith helmet, and where would Marconi, Edison, Salk, Pasteur and others be if they hid their talents under a bushel.

*

There are many ways to show off your ability, and still not be a show-off.

Get Off the Back Porch!

The tragedy in life is to see some expert too shy a guy to get places. "If only somebody knew of his talent," say his friends, adding, "but old Phil prefers to sit quietly at parties and smoke his pipe in a corner. He's the back porch introvert in life, not the extrovert on the front porch waving at all who go by."

One stratagem to gain attention if you aren't the talkative type yourself is the old trick of being a good listener.

Show interest in others, and you'll attract as much attention as the talker.

Be quick to say, "It's interesting. Please go on."

That talker then really sees you, for you are an admirer, and who can help but remember the face of an admirer who is sincere?

No boss can resist such temptation.

The poor listener is one whose eyes wander as you talk;

who makes you feel you are boring him, or that he can't wait until you stop talking so he can let loose himself.

Never be quick to put words in others' mouths. This disconcerts them no end. They are struggling to find the right word, and you put it right into their mouths for them. This makes them feel inferior to you; and soon you won't be "seen" much by that person. He doesn't want an egg-head around to put words in *his* mouth.

So let the other person have the fun of groping for words. Lean toward him physically and mentally, and grasp his every word. Then if you are a conversationalist yourself, do as the Maynard brothers do, and tactfully weave the conversation from points you are weak in to your own strong points, then let loose. Don't hide behind a false shyness.

Be a good listener first—but when it is your turn, *be a good talker.*

CHAPTER THOUGHT

People who hide on the back porches of life get no place. Those who get places use such strategy and sizzlemanship as:

1. Learn ways to be "seen" and "heard."
2. Attract attention in a dignified way.
3. Show off your talents, but don't be a show-off.
4. Be the good listener *first,* the good talker *second.*

"Don't Take Your Ability for Granted"

Poor Elmer's Own Almanac
Of Proverbs

1. "What Is There In It—For The Other Fellow?"
2. "You Must Mean Business To Do Business."
3. "Get Along With Others—and You'll Get Along!"
4. "Have a Target In Life To Aim At."
5. "You Can Get Anywhere By Starting Where You Are."
6. "Everything Becomes Easy When You Have KNOW HOW."
7. "Sometimes I Find It Pays To Be Ignorant!"
8. "You Must Prepare For Luck And Breaks!"
9. "When You Fall Learn How To Bounce!"

From my book, "The Wealth Within You."

11

If you really want
to get along with people,
pick the right day to ask them for favors,
for weather does affect
the moods of mankind

*"Everybody talks about it—but no one
does anything about it—well, very few people."*

I asked Jasmine Chan of Hong Kong, who was dining with
me and Tony Pfiffner and others at the Miramar Hotel's Chinese Room, "How come the people of Hong Kong move so
fast? Like New Yorkers, they are quick to give assent in closing a deal."

Jasmine, who is running her late husband's business, said,
"It is the Chinese who move fast—not others. The Chinese
are like New Yorkers, and when the air is brisk, so are they."

"You mean the air makes people move fast or slow, and
also affects their speed of saying yes or no in deals?" I chal-
lenged.

"Indeed, yes," said this brilliant widow who was so ably
running her husband's business. "There is a right time of the
day, as well as the week or month, to ask favors of others."

I expected to hear something about star reading, but R. N.
Kaul of Air India arrived, and hearing our discussion, added

119

this statement: "I have noted on muggy, humid days in HK, or elsewhere in the world, that people do react with the weather. They are inclined to slow up when the weather is heavy, and to move fast when it has a light moisture content. If I wished to win over someone on an important issue, I'd pick a brisk, clear day—one that is preferably sunny and cheerful, for the weather will react on the person I want to convince. It will put that person in a receptive mood."

"You mean people get along with each other better on days with low humidity?"

Kaul said it was true. Jasmine nodded. Pfiffner agreed as Kaul gave examples of the high humidity of port cities, as an example, and how difficult it was to get people to sit down for a conversation, let alone to get a decision out of them. "They grunt on humid days," observed Kaul. "These are days for only old and reliable friends to get together."

"I have noted the same thing," said Pfiffner. "When the barometer is rising so are people's spirits. This puts them into a friendly frame of mind."

Watch the Barometer

About this time another world traveler, Fred Clemo, came up and said: "Perhaps we should look at the barometer each morning, rather than our sales manuals, to see how to sell that day. If we pick the wrong barometer reading, then we show a loss of profits and friendships for the day. Right?"

"Right-o," said Pfiffner, and I saw the others rather agreed with Clemo.

"I find the best time of day to make friends," added Jasmine, "is in the cool of the morning. With the sun still not too hot, and the breeze still cool and dew-fragrant from the night before, people are easier to sell. They respond better over a cup of morning tea."

"Ah," I said, "you give me an idea: that friendships should be made early in the day."

"Or in the evening," winked Pfiffner.

This conversation sounds as if one were being joshed, but it is not so. The Orientals know the value of weather in making history. They plan their big and little compaigns for the cool of the day, when the humidity is right. Centuries ago men and women always consulted a star gazer, so to speak, for advice on when and what to do. Without knowing so, perhaps many a reader of the stars advised people to do things on "clear, sunny days" and to save the "humid days for old friends only."

I saw how true this could be. As a salesman once myself (I guess I'm still one, as are we all), I kept away from business prospects on rainy, dull and dead days. I avoided them on Monday morning after a big week-end, when their spirits were low. I avoided them on Friday afternoons for they had their minds on week-end pleasures, not on buying newspaper space from me or the vacuum cleaner I once sold. Instinctively, I was picking and choosing the right time of day and the right kind of weather to make my calls.

"I guess you might say," put in Tony Pfiffner, a sales agent for Swissair, "that days of the month when bills are due are also bad days to get money or agreements from others. And it might well be said that certain times of the year (income-tax time, Christmas for example), are bad times to ask people to part with money even for travel tickets. Fund raisers know this and time their calls to certain slack seasons. Indeed, there are definite times of day, week, month and year to ask favors of others."

*

Later I had a similar conversation with Don Wilson and Gordon McCoun, men with Panagra Airlines that fly to South

America, and again I learned that when days were murky, say, in Peru, or the festivities were on in Rio, that business just about folded up. Instinctively, intelligent businessmen avoid these times.

Ancient medicine knew this. That is why they advised so accurately when to start a battle, when to start any campaign, even when to get married.

Instinctively (or from bitter experience) wives know better than to spring the idea of a new dress purchase on hubby before breakfast, or on dull days when the old boy is not in good spirits. After dinner or on a sunny day is the time to approach hubby about that dress.

Use Good Timing

A good employee knows the time of day to approach the boss for a raise, and certainly that isn't until after the mail has been dealt with, and the boss is more relaxed. A good time is when he has just returned from a vacation, all pepped up and in good spirits.

Proper timing is important in making friends, in promoting ideas, and in asking favors.

*

Now this all might sound pseudo-scientific.

It did to me until I got some real scientific information from the Carrier Corporation, "makers of weather." They informed me that, scientifically, weather does affect people mentally and physically, and they went one step further by saying that people can control the weather in a business conference to make certain that people will respond favorably to requests. In particular I talked with a Bill McKenna and Al Walker of this firm of weathermakers, and was greatly enlightened.

"Take August," said Walker, "the police have always called it the month of murders, for the heat and heavy humidity of this month make people growl at one another and at the smallest annoyance that would never bother them in December. In the hot months people fly off the handle quicker. So I'd certainly avoid the hot, humid months—unless, of course, I could meet in an air conditioned room."

McKenna added: "Naturally all humid days aren't murderous days—nor all crisp days made for Pollyanna, but weather does affect the organs of the body and especially the brain. When weather is heavy it actually depresses the head, and your brain is depressed and is groggy. On light, airy days the weather doesn't weigh down on the head, and people function better."

These were well taken points about human relations.

"But how does weather actually affect people?" I asked.

I was then given a lesson in "ions."

I was quoted this paragraph from an issue of *House Beautiful:*

"The air you breathe has electrical charges. These electrically charged particles are called Ions. Some of them are negatively charged, other have positive ions. The amount of ratio between negative ions and positive ions in the air you breathe apparently affects how you feel."

It is therefore scientifically known now that air filled with *negative ions* raises spirits of people. Which is why artificial air conditioning livens people even on muggy days outside; for it puts negative ions into a room for our comfort.

The Winds of Chance

It is a known fact that the ill-fated Foehn winds of the Alps, the Mistral winds of France and our own Chinook winds off the Rocky Mountains, loaded with positive ions, cause all sorts of discomforts to people and make them irritable and in no mood for making friends or spending money.

This is no idle statement—but a scientific fact.

Rooms, too, can produce their own Chinook winds.

The rule, therefore, when asking favors is to choose a time when the negative ions are at their highest percent in the atmosphere.

Dr. Albert P. Krueger, professor emeritus of bacteriology, and R. F. Smith, both of the University of California, found that air high in negative ions makes mucus flow in our nose. In so doing it clears the nasal passages of polution just as an air conditioner in a room does—giving us our own air conditioning unit.

Dr. Igho Kornbluch of the University of Pennsylvania says negative ions give us a nice tranquilizing effect, and reduce high blood pressure. So if you have a proposal that might raise the blood pressure of someone, pick a day high in negative ions! Silly? Well, I don't think so.

Absenteeism is at a minimum, according to the American Institute of Medical Climatology in Philadelphia, when the weather is properly filled with negative ions.

Well, so much for the scientific side of weather and its use in helping you win friendships and getting others to agree to your way of thinking.

*

Here, now, is practical information from more world travelers, men with practical experience:

On a recent world trip I asked Spiro Varvias of Cairo why his city had a fast pace similar to New York City's, and he told me the same story: "It is our climate. It is dry here, usually free of sweat and humidity, permitting people to walk fast and move around without being uncomfortable as in some city such as New Orleans that is moist and humid."

I approached Enrique Marsans of Madrid at the ASTA

convention of travel agents one day, along with Flandrac of Paris and Bill Turner of Tokyo, all of whom responded to my quest for information and its effect on people.

Marsans spoke first: "Madrid is a fast-moving city, for it is usually dry. But Barcelona is humid and people move slower and respond with less enthusiasm to business requests. Our wild Flamenco dancers come from our hilly land, where it is high and dry and gives a brisk zest to life. When you say 'the languid Spaniard,' you must qualify the region of his home, for climate makes people alert and alive or moody and mellow."

Bill Turner said of Tokyo: "We have yearly climatic changes from hot to cold as in the United States. These changes keep people on their toes. That is why Tokyo has fast-moving feet, yet the Japanese in humid Singapore take things easier and are slower to respond."

Flandrac of Paris said: "I am cautious where I send travelers. You can't sell trips to Nice when the weather there is hot. People are content to remain in Paris. But when cold weather comes, ah, then Nice looks nice. You see, to be a good agent you must go along with the weather."

Gluck, also of Paris, came up at this moment, and he nodded in agreement to his compatriot, adding, "Morning is the time to sell travel tickets. For when the weather is cool and pleasant, so are ticket buyers. My business has its daily ups and downs, following the weather changes. Certainly I have my high months every year, and make my plans around these months of the year. I watch calendar and barometer and thermometer and act accordingly."

Blowing Hot and Cold

And so it went—wherever I visited around the world I found people reacting to the weather. In bazaars, flea and thieve's markets—in little shops and in big stores. In offices and show rooms and in homes, in each I saw that weather made friends or lost them. It might well be scientifically stated: *"According to the number of negative ions, people loosen their hearts for friendships and their purse strings for purchases."*

People do "blow hot and cold" with the ions!

*

In Naples one day I was told by the Aloschi Brothers, also travel agents dependent on people's moods, that Naples produced the romantic songs of Italy, for the climate is warm there and conducive to songs of love, while in northern Milan people have less time for singing but more for business.

One of the Alochi Brothers told me, "A man of Milan will forego a good meal to own a business suit. A man of Rome will forego a business suit for a good meal—while the man of Naples will forego both the suit and the meal if he can have a hammock, a guitar and time to think what he'd do if he had the business suit and the good meal."

Hilda Steinle of Athens once told me: "The bright sun of Greece, the lack of much humidity, has made this land a place where, when Greek meets Greek, they don't sing songs, but start a business!"

So it went world wide: India, Lebanon, Germany, England —all lands are affected by natural weather, and their speed of action reflected in the climate of the moment. Indeed, by proper timing suitable to the climate of the land you can control your relationships with the people you meet and know.

Here is how to find the most congenial time of the day, week or month to puruse friends and business acquaintances. Make a list such as the following:

> Happy days
> Cheerful days
> Pleasant days

Fair days
Poor days
Neutral days
Unpleasant days
Blue days
Depressed days
Sour days
Gay days

Now study your own daily, weekly and monthly ups and downs. Chart yourself accordingly, and you'll be amazed to learn you, too, have a pattern of ups and downs that can be used to your advantage in winning others over.

To make this personal study more custom-tailored to yourself, note the exact day and date opposite each of the above reactions. Do so for an entire year, and you'll wake up to find you have a real Weather Chart, made-to-measure for your own self that you can use when going out to make friends or deals.

If the pattern becomes clear, for example, that Monday is your "Blue Day," then do office work or keep away from people. When you learn that spring is your best time of year, plan your big events for that season. If August is your down month, take your vacation.

"Know thyself."

Understand your own moods and whims, and then you'll begin to understand those of others and fit your plans into their moods. Chances are if certain days are your Blue Days, you'll find others similarly affected.

Find your weather cycle—and you'll find a scientific basis for success.

P.S. Watch your ions!

Who's The Author?

Hearts like doors,
Can open with ease
To very, very little Keys;
And don't forget that two of these
Are "Thank you, sir," and "If you
　　please."

Chabliss T. Dean heard this back in 1905 and has been quoting it ever since to make life easier for himself. Who is the author, he asks?

You see, if you thank people and say please, they are less grumpy with you. You get along smoother, are less annoyed and upset, burn up less energy and look younger.

Politeness saves energy—keeps us youthful.

Who wrote all this? Who is the author?

When A Story Is Being Told Relax And Live Longer

It is a great temptation, when someone is telling a funny story, to interrupt with a shout, "Aw, that's an old one!" When you interrupt a person, you make an enemy—and burn up needless energy.

When a joke or amusing story is being told, relax, listen and enjoy it. Remember, the other fellow gets fun out of telling it. Let him have his fun. He'll like you better, and you've golden time to relax and live longer.

12

The hypnotist's great secret
that anyone can use
to influence people to
your way of thinking

"No one knows what he can do until he tries it."

One day I watched a professor open a bottle and say to his students, "As soon as you smell the lilac perfume raise your hands."

Soon half the class had raised its hands.

Yet it was a bottle of plain colored water.

I have seen people blind-folded at parties and told they would be asked to hold a hot poker. When a piece of ordinary ice was suddenly placed into their hands, they screamed.

In similar tests teachers have held a hand to one ear and have said, "Hear the bee buzzing?"

Many students raised their hands.

*

What is the psychology behind these simple tests?

This: that the "seller" of the idea has put the idea into

129

your mind, *subconsciously,* and has hypnotized you into be-
lieving what he has said.

It is an ancient method of influencing people.

It is one you can use to assure any image you'd like to
project.

*

A tactful boss says, "Your desk will have more light and
privacy over there, don't you think?", and the employee
agrees. A positive idea has been put into his head.

You can insert many ideas into the minds of others through
this method of the hypnotists. You can put customers or
friends into a "trance" if you use the proper words.

Just make sure that your ideas are honest and believable.
Don't try to sell comfort that you know is lacking, or light
that you know is not available in the corner. Be honest.

Use Word Pictures

Pick out points you want to get across to others. Dramatize
these points with word pictures, always being positive in your
language. "This luggage will withstand a 300 foot fall," says
one seller, for that is true of fiberglass luggage. Another says,
"This new frying pan needs no grease—even eggs will not
stick." That is the truth.

As you speak to others, further "hypnotize" them by nodding your head up and down, positively, to get their heads
nodding. It is difficult to say the word "No" when your head
is nodding up and down. Test yourself.

Getting people to nod through use of positive language, is
the monkey-see, monkey-do technique. It works with most
people.

You will observe the technique at all auctions. The auctioneer is always nodding his head up and down to inspire others to do likewise.

*

It is often claimed that close to 99% of our beliefs and habits are the result, not of having thought the matter out for ourselves, but of suggestions coming positively from others.

Evangelists sell in this manner to the masses; so do governments. It is a favorite trick of all dictators and propagandists.

You, too, can use the principle to sell your honest ideas to others.

Harry Baldwin, the airline man, never says of a new jet, "Do you think jets are quiet?" He is more positive. He wants to get a true image across, so nods his head up and down as he says, "Listen—aren't these jets quiet?" The passengers hear only *silence*.

That's the great power of positive language.

CHAPTER THOUGHT

Be positive in all you do and say; and you will win others over to your way of thinking. Find the image you'd like to sell to others, then nod them into a "buying trance."

The Five Friend-Makers

Several years ago, through my sales training institute, I put out a pocket-size card listing my five Friend-makers. *Tide Magazine* reprinted the card. Then *Reader's Digest*. Soon it had thousands of reprints circulating around the world, so I offer the content of the card to you. It will be of great value in helping you to get along with people, and go places faster in life:

1. "I am proud of you!" The 5 best words to make people feel good. Try them on the boss, employee, wife, husband, friend. You elevate their ego—and they'll never let you down.
2. "What is YOUR opinion?" The 4 greatest words to gain willing information, from the toughest person or utter stranger. You compliment their judgment. They like that.
3. "If you please!" Three magic words to get fast action out of people for the things and favors you ask of them. Tag this on all requests.
4. "Thank you!" Two words to make people glad they did a favor. Never fail to use them. "Thank you" is in every language.
5. "YOU!!" The one word to make the most friends. People like to hear about THEMSELVES. So use YOU—never "I", the smallest word in the world.

13

How to get
the full attention of people
so they really sit up and
actually "hear" and "see" you

"Two good talkers are not worth one good listener."

Liberace, the piano player, once was asked, "Why the candelabra on the piano each time you give a concert?"

"To gain attention," was Liberace's simple answer.

"And the fancy clothes? Also to attract attention?"

"Yes," said Liberace, "and my piano-shaped swimming pool—they are all my attention-getters."

"Don't you feel," he was further asked, "that your good music is enough of an attention getter without the need for a candelabra on the piano?"

"To gain attention to good music," explained Liberace, "you must have a gimmick,—something unusual that has *remembrance value* and at once identifies you. One day a candelabra was accidently placed on my piano. It softened my audience. They like me very much that night."

Then Liberace told how one night he felt the need to attract attention to himself while conducting an orchestra in the Hollywood Bowl. "All my musicians wore black tails. So I put on white tails to be easily identified. I went to Las Vegas and the producer there asked what gimmick I had. I told him about the white tails. He told me that was old, to get something new. And so it went, each place wanted a new dress gimmick—and I had to top myself."

Indeed, Liberace did top himself at a command performance before Queen Elizabeth. "I wore a diamond-studded jacket. It cost $10,000, but of course the ticket buyers paid for it," said Liberace, a smile in his eyes, for it has often been said by his critics, "Liberace laughs all the way to the bank."

Showmanship in Your Life

Liberace is a showman. He knows the value of attention-getting, to prevent being lost on the stage—or forgotten after the performance.

You say this is fine for the theatre—but not the business world?

Maybe.

But Liberace realized that his Hollywood home had attracted attention. He observed people peeking over the fence, even climbing it, to see his famous piano-shaped pool. So he went into the real-estate business by building homes with piano-shaped pools. Then apartment houses.

Silly? Ridiculous?

Well, they say Liberace now walks to the bank laughing as he carries his money bags!

Do People Really "Hear" You?

Often people fail to "hear" you because you haven't caught their inner attention. They are looking at you—but not hearing you.

Often, too, people can stare right at you and never "see" you.

That's bad. You seem to melt into the surroundings. People will say a week later, "Oh, were you at Jim's party? I didn't see you."

This is enough to make anyone feel unimportant and unneeded.

Yet the cure is simple: *gain attention.*

Maybe attention can be secured through some sartorial effect: a carnation in the lapel, an unusual cigarette holder, or a fashion sense that makes you stand out.

Failing the sartorial ability to attract attention, then perhaps you can use your ability to engage in a lively conversation.

Acquire a knack for telling stories; or better yet, by being a good listener, become a merry and pleasant audience for others.

Showmanship in Business

Retailers put unusual prices on merchandise to attract attention. First it was the nine series, 9¢ 19¢ 99¢, $1.39, $1.99 and so forth. These figures looked like good bargains and caught the eye of casual passersby.

Now the eight series is popular. 8¢, 18¢, 88¢ and so forth.

People used to seeing the nine figures suddenly "saw" the eight figures, and were attracted.

A person sends a dollar bill to a prospect saying, "I'd like to buy $1.00 of your time. May I?" That letter gains attention.

Volkswagen is the biggest selling foreign car in the United States. Their advertisements gain attention first through the use of large white space. coupled with short, clever headlines telling the public such amusing things as "no style changes in years—yet 57 invisible changes for improvement this year alone."

Rolls-Royce attracts attention to the quality of the entire car through the clock. Their advertisements (and their dealers), will tell you, "The clock is the noisiest part of the car, but our engineers are working on it."

Metzger's Dairy in Dallas has a man appearing on TV saying, "For the next minute I will ask you to concentrate on my product. It's a test of your extra sensory perception." You see Metzger's name for a fleeting second as he starts to invite you to watch. Then he closes his eyes and keeps them closed for one minute while you watch with full attention. No commercial is given, but he knows you are repeating to yourself, "Metzger Dairies."

Metzger's newspaper advertisements at times take five half columns, with just their name, in small, 10 point print, in the very center of the island of white.

That's gaining attention.

A door-to-door seller greets the housewife by saying, "Hasn't this perfume a lovely new aroma?"

He opens the bottle, smells it himself to get the monkey-see, monkey-do instinct working, and then hands the bottle to the woman. What woman can resist smelling a new perfume?

Another salesman raps at the door. When the woman comes he hands her a "Free brush, madam, for your use."

All are commercial ways to gain rapid attention.

Social Showmanship

Socially, a hostess has a rare facility in choosing slacks, or perhaps she plays unusual background music, say from India. She may serve a course of some unusual food each time you visit her. That's her trade mark, her way of gaining attention as a hostess by giving her guests a reason to remember their visit.

One way to gain attention is to invite someone into another room. "I have something important to tell you." They are then all ears and eyes.

One friend of ours grows only white flowers in the yard.

Another I know has a garden using one type of flower in great masses—this is a striking way to gain attention to yourself and your home.

People Like to Be Heard

People want to be recognized.

They want to be seen and heard—not just looked at with a deaf ear aimed at them, but that is hearing someone else in the room.

People hate to speak and not be heard.

Public speakers often have gimmicks to gain the immediate attention of an audience. They may hold something high over their head. They may open with an unusual but striking statement such as, "Five of you will be dead from heart attacks by January!"

A child rides a bike in front of his parents and shouts, "Look—no hands." This startling demonstration scares his parents into full attention.

Perhaps the greatest desire of all humanity is to gain attentive respect.

Russia sends a man around the world in outer space to gain attention. One world leader took off a shoe and banged it on his desk at the United Nations. This may not have been good Emily Post, but it gained attention.

Castro ate chickens in his room when he visited New York City. His men wear fatigue clothes and beards. Can you imagine Castro without a beard? He'd look too ordinary.

Teddy Roosevelt wore a campaign hat, glasses, and a broad grin to gain attention to his antics.

One world leader wore a table cloth. Another a fez hat.

When they entered a room, they got attention.

But Don't Over-Do It

However, a warning.

Don't over-do attention getting to a point you are considered exotic. A queer one. That's carrying the attention-getting too far. Learn the delicate touches of dress and speech.

Have good manners.

William Gilmore Simms advocates, "The only true source of politeness is consideration."

A person who shows consideration, gains attention.

An attentive person gains attention.

"Nothing except what flows from the heart can render even external manners truly pleasing," says the great Hugh Blair. So let your attention be sincere.

"We cannot always oblige," said Voltaire, "but we can always speak obligingly."

What better way can you use to gain honest attention than by a pleasant attitude toward others through politeness and fine manners?

Try "An Inch of Politeness"

The Chinese say, "An inch of gold cannot purchase an inch of time."

But an inch of politeness and a pleasant expression can gain hours of another's time, attention and interest in you.

Learn the social amenity of phoning people after they've entertained you. Say how good it was. Learn to write "thank you" letters, and people will want you to return. As one philosopher says, "Learn to handle a writing brush . . . and you'll never handle a begging bowl."

One Thing to Avoid

Avoid gossiping.

People who fail to gossip, attract attention.

"Beware of too much talk." Especially about people not present.

And before you say something that may be taken wrongly, "take a second look . . . it costs you nothing."

Be short on bragging about your wealth. That is no attention-getter. It keeps people away from your hearth in envy and jealousy of you. Remember, "riches add to the house . . . virtues to the man."

Be wary of too much self-praise. It may identify you, yes— but as a bore, or an insincere person trying to win friendships.

Don't be a doubting Thomas, always skeptical of what others say and do.

Again from the Chinese comes this philosophy, "Better to believe too much than nothing at all."

Give others benefit of the doubt.

When you appear doubting, act doubting, say doubting things, you lose friendships fast. Talk little of doubt—for water and words are easy to pour, impossible to recover.

Think twice before criticizing—then don't say it.

The Big Rule to Use

The world is hungry for attention.

People crave others to sit and listen to them.

The rule for gaining attention is to be attentive yourself.

You may wish to gain attention through dress or social accomplishments—or you may prefer to gain it by being a good audience to others.

Learn, too, the art of saying what interests others.

Always remember the oriental motto: "Scholars talk books —butchers talk pigs."

CHAPTER THOUGHT

If you would seek attention, first give attention. If you want to dine at a friend's home, don't insult the cook. A good friend is a found treasure. Two good talkers are not worth one good listener.

THE ART OF
MAKING 'EM THIRSTY

From my most successful book, *How To Sell Yourself To Others* (Prentice-Hall, Inc.), I listed one of the many formulas that I developed to help people go places in life. This formula has been reproduced by publishers in many countries. It seems to work in all languages:

"MAKE 'EM THIRSTY" CARD

1. **DON'T MAKE 'EM DRINK . . . MAKE 'EM THIRSTY:** If you will make people thirsty for you they will be your greatest friends. Don't drive people . . . lead them. Make them "thirsty" and "hungry" for your friendship.
2. **DON'T SELL AN EMPTY BOX:** Here is one way to make people "thirsty." Always do more for them than you expect in return. Grab bags often disappoint . . . so make your box of goodwill chock-full. Give **MORE** than you receive.
3. **GET IN STEP WITH OTHERS:** Another fine way to make people "hungry" for your friendship. The secret is to learn their hobbies, interests and emotions . . . then fall in step with them. Don't force them to get in step with you.
4. **IF YOU CAN'T CONVINCE 'EM, JOIN 'EM:** You'll never lose a balking friend if you join forces with him especially when you see he won't be convinced. Often by retracting a little at first, you go further in the long run.

14

Try this magic formula: have
a genuine regard for others—
and in so doing, have many friends

"The tongue, like a sharp knife . . .
kills without drawing blood."

I asked Clarence Talley what his secret of success might be.
Talley is one of the lucky people who "discovered" the
Volkswagen early enough to get in on the kill, so to speak;
by recognizing the car as one the people of the U. S. wanted,
he opened an agency in Dallas long before the "Volks rush"
started.

Clarence told me the reason he got along with people was
his great regard for others.

"Regard?" I asked. "Please explain."

"I mean I treat others as if they were members of my
family. As if they were members of my choice club in Dallas,
the famed Exhausted Roosters. I treat all people with regard."

"Then people like this feeling strongly enough to buy a
foreign made car?" I asked.

"Yes," he said, "but please don't call them foreign cars.

They are *imported* cars. It is a better choice of words. You'd never call scotch a foreign drink. It's an import from Scotland."

I saw Talley's thinking. I agreed with it. I agreed further when he said: "When I give a man an appraisal on his car, I never kick his tires, nor do I observe scratches on the body. I nod in respect of his car. I regard it as a good possession of his, and in not belittling his car I gain the man's respect."

A person has good manners when he can put up with someone who has bad manners.

Be Considerate of Others

It might be another way of saying, "Have good manners."

It would not be good manners to criticize others publicly; to belittle their possessions; to sniff at their offers; to scoff at their remarks.

If you are considerate of others' feelings, if you regard their silliest wish with respect, you will gain respect.

The one quality that makes the gentleman is his sensibilities for others.

Your feelings toward others should be keen. Then you will observe their thoughts, and respect them even if you disagree with them.

Learn to Hold Your Tongue

Another trait to help you to win others over is to learn how to hold your tongue.

"When a customer comes storming into my place," says Talley, "and sets up a fuss, I hold my tongue. I can remember one chap only yesterday. He had a grievance, and expected me to blow up in his face. I didn't. I listened to him. I respected his complaint. I held my tongue. You know what he finally said?"

"No," I said, "but I'll bet you won him over."

" 'Talley'," said the griper, " 'why aren't you mad? Why aren't you kicking me out? I thought I'd rile you up, but you are holding back your feelings. I respect you.' "

Talley won the man over by the one great trait that is so hard for many of us to learn: *the ability to hold our tongue.*

As the Chinese merchant says, "Soft tongue stays . . . hard teeth fall."

Remember, it is hard to keep your mouth and your mind open at the same time.

Give and You'll Get

Too often politeness means: I want something.

Too often the man with his hat in his hand, humbly visiting with you, is about to beg for something.

But the worst of the lot is the one who fails to hold his tongue and blows his top.

If you always give—you'll always have.

Give with consideration and politeness, especially to angry people, and you'll gain their respectful regard.

Quickly Admit You Are Wrong

Another trick to win others is: *blame yourself as you blame others . . . forgive others as you forgive yourself.*

Buddha couldn't have put it better.

It is a truism of business and social contacts to be first to admit you are wrong, for in so doing you rob the other person of a chance to say you are in error.

It is better to say, "I admit I failed to understand you clearly," than to shout, "I hear you—and you are all wrong!"

A Virtue of Disraeli

"Guarding the tongue" is a virtue that Disraeli, the Jew, had in days when he needed to hold his tongue against very severe and impolite critics.

Disraeli's trick was to disregard the fire of the other.

Do the same. Fail to hear "the fire." Let it hit and pass. Roll with the blows. Remember, sticks and stones break bones but words never do.

Words may break the spirit of the other. For they fly heedlessly out of your mouth, and unlike a letter, cannot be erased from the air.

Once when Stanton wanted to cause Lincoln to blow up, he called him a fool. Lincoln, as the famous story goes, never "heard" the word fool. He saved his face by not hearing it, and this disconcerted Stanton who finally gave in when Lincoln remarked, innocuously, *Stanton is usually right.*

*

Words spoken in haste have no place in the business world.

Business can't always run smoothly. But when it fails to, and someone seeks to blame you, try Lincoln's psychology and say, "I am sure you are right."

Then go on to state your own case.

*

Remember Emerson's line: "No man has a prosperity so high or firm, but that two or three words can dishearten it, and there is no calamity which right words will not begin to redress."

Watch Your Every Word

Words are like dynamite.

They can cause explosions.

Words spoken in haste make others doubly angry.

Abbott and Costello, Weber and Fields, Laurel and Hardy, Jerry Lewis and Dean Martin, were once great teams.

Did they fall apart for lack of talent?

No—rather for lack of the one great acting skill—holding the tongue in place.

For you can't erase the spoken word.

Don't Use Idle Words

The high caste Hindu, I learned in visiting India, has one motto: he takes an oath not to use words *idly*.

Read Zen and Tao and the writings of Buddha, and you will see what I mean, for the Hindus fail to gossip.

As said by Douglas Jerrol (and by Clarence Talley), "The last word is the most dangerous of infernal machines."

Husbands and wives realize this (or should).

So should people who gossip.

The one who gossips . . . the one who has the last word . . . is on his last friends.

For "the swiftest horse can't overtake the spoken word."

A Good Formula

1. Show great regard for others.
2. Be sensitive to the feelings of the people around you.
3. Learn to hold your tongue.
4. Never gossip.
5. Let others have the last word.

"With true friends even water drunk together is sweet enough."

A Short, Short Story

You'll Never Make An Enemy With This One Simple Rule

Never blow your horn needlessly!

By this I mean never blow off in front of people, or for that matter in back of them.

More ill-will is gained by sounding off your "horn" than in any other way I know—especially when you are in the driver's seat.

The rule is to have good manners.

Good manners includes not blowing a horn at people who are slow on the take-off. Learn to relax in the driver's seat of life. Only too often a mild-mannered person with lots of "sorry" and "please" and "thank you" in the living room becomes a tyrant driving on the street.

The person whom you blow your horn at might be your next customer, a present client, the wife of the boss, a friend of a friend or a deputy sheriff on his day off. You are taking chances blowing horns at people's rears!

Remember the rule: *use good manners!*

> *"Here lies the body of William Jay,*
> *Who died maintaining his right of way—*
> *He was right, dead right, as he sped along,*
> *But he's just as dead as if he were wrong."*
> Boston Transcript

15

How to gain popularity

A short, short story.

What is popularity?

The girl at school asks, "Is he popular?"

The boy at school asks, "Is she popular?"

One presidential candidate wins over another because of his "great popularity." A business man promotes an employee because "He's popular with the staff."

What is popularity?

First, it isn't education. Often the person who tries to be smart, is disliked. He's called an "egg head."

Second, popularity isn't money—nor possessions. Many a rich man is the most unpopular man in the community.

Third, popularity isn't being talented or skilled. Many a concert pianist lacks the popularity of a Jack Benny.

A little puppy dog can be popular—for he is friendly, playful, easy to get along with, and is a good listener, never criticizes, just grins. He knows when to relax and just look at you. He's no bother.

This popularity can be acquired.

No practice is necessary in a school. For often it doesn't come from formal schooling. It comes from a desire to want to get along with the people around you.

Here are some rules for being popular:

1. Listen more than you talk.
2. Withhold criticism of others.
3. Be quick to join in on the fun.
4. Don't be a know-it-all.
5. Don't lord it over the underdog.
6. Don't be Mr. Perfection.
7. Admit you may be wrong.

"Hide your offended heart . . . keep your valued friends."

P.S.: We all like lamb . . . each has a different way of cooking it . . . and his way must be respected!

How Old Is Old?

You'd never guess the age of the woman who has played opposite such leading men as Gable, Boyer, Cooper, Heflin, Taylor, Wayne, Brent, Milland, McLaglen, starring in *Sorry, Wrong Number, Double Indemnity, Stella Dallas* and innumerable other movies. Today she has her own TV program!

Yet this female Bob Cummings is 54—and still a glamorous star.

She is Barbara Stanwyck.

When, then, is a person old?

The answer seems to be: "Anyone ten years older than I am is an old person!"

In fact, anyone one year older than my own teenager, is "an old person."

16

"Thank you" and "if you please"
are two ways to
make new friends and
to hold the friends you now have

"When the mind becomes large, the speech becomes simple."

Recently Harry Rolnick, Mr. Hat in the hat manufacturing business, was given what is perhaps the world's greatest designer's acclaim: the famed Neiman Marcus Award for outstanding design in the hat field.

I asked the president of his firm, Ken Jewell, how "neighbor Harry" became so famous.

"He came to the Southwest as a young fellow from Brooklyn and began cleaning hats," said Jewell. "He found two secrets: he'd say 'thank you' and 'if you please.'"

"You mean that was his formula for building Byer-Rolnick into one of the largest hat factories in the world?" I asked him.

"Indeed, yes," said Jewell. "Never once did he let a customer leave without two words, 'Thank you.' Only Harry made the words bow from the hips. He didn't say them just from the lips—but bowed them from the hips."

I liked that idea.

Too many people mumble a mechanical "thanks," but obviously this man knew the art of making his "thank you" come from the hips—not the lips.

Try Bob Roth's Technique

I recall many a popular man who has told me, "I always say, 'if you please' in asking favors of another person. Even the humblest person likes to hear 'if you please.'"

Bob Roth once told me: "I even thank a waiter . . . and am quick to say 'If you please' when I ask for even a napkin or fork. It makes the fellow feel important. I find it helps greatly in dealing with all service people. When you say 'if you please,' the service station attendant does a better cleaning job on my car window, the elevator operator is more pleasant when I say 'if you please' to him, and so on down the line. People feel important when you add 'if you please' to your request."

Become "Thank You" Conscious

During the last world war I wrote an article, "Take an Hour to Say No."

The idea was to hesitate before you shout, "I'm all sold out—don't you know there is a war on?"

The article was intended to build future goodwill for sellers and business houses by encouraging them to pause before shouting "NO" about the availability of an item hard to get in wartime.

Cadillac Motors printed the booklet in a black note book and called it *Elmer's Little Black Notebook*. Other firms wrote for permission to print it. Finally over 200 firms re-printed the booklet 70,000,000 times!

The effect was tremendous.

The world suddenly became "thank you" conscious.

People really started to take an hour before they yelled "NO" to others, and things softened up.

The formula can still work today.

Make It a Sad "No"

If you have no rooms left in your hotel, don't shout, "ALL SOLD OUT—SORRY."

If you are over-sold on anything, "Hesitate—a long while —and then make it a sad 'No.' "

Be sorry for the other person. Weep with him. In fact, weep until the person says, "Say, don't take it so hard. I'll be back when you get your stock up again."

Take out a handkerchief. Be sad. Look sad. Weep.

That's the way to make friends, not enemies, in this world of ours.

*

Learn the great friend-making quality of "Thank you" and "If you please," two phrases that will carry you far in life.

I'm a fall guy myself for "Thank you" and "if you please." So are others.

Thank You World Wide

Here is how to say thank you in several languages.

Muchas gracias	Merci beaucoup
Danke schön	Koszonom
Tak skal de ha	Bardzo dzkuje
Dankbetuiging	Grazie

So to get places fast with others, say "thank you." The wife, the husband, the children, the neighbors, the milkman, all like to hear "thank you" for the favor they've done.

The boss, the employee—the people who call on you, never like to be ordered around, or to be told to do something without your adding, *"—if you please."*

It's the sugar coating that helps them to do things willingly, energetically, and gladly.

Good Manners Never Go Out Of Style.

TRICKS TO BE A
HUSBAND (OR WIFE)-KEEPER

1. Listen well.
2. Listen often.
3. Listen long.
4. Listen intently.
5. Listen avidly.
6. Listen.

17

One big word
that will take you fast
down any road to success
that you care to pick

"In the presence of princes the cleverest jester is mute."

Civility is the word.
Civility—meaning "being nice to people."

*

George is a waiter at the Dallas Athletic Club. He waits on our group called The Round Table.

At times he forgets the salt, and the sugar is often out of reach—but George is never out of reach when it comes to responding to simple civility.

In particular, there is the "head man" at our table, called The Bishop. J. W. Blanton is hugging 100, but seldom misses a meal at the table.

As he starts across the dining room to the table, George has his seat all ready for him. When "Bishop" Blanton gets ready to leave, George gets his walking stick, and takes him to the elevator. Downstairs one or more bellboys not only

help him to the door—but across the busy street to his office.
That's civility!

*

"Kindness is the only service that power cannot command and money cannot buy," says an old Serbian proverb.

George never read the proverb. But he knew the principle instinctively.

The Oriental Way

"Hide your offended heart—keep your valued friends."
That's how it is done in the Orient.

When one is hurt, especially unintentionally, don't let it show even in your eyes.

You must learn not to injure people accidentally, even by a glance.

Cast your eyes another way. Overlook the ailment of others.

Be quick to change the subject matter from one that offends others, to one that is neutral.

*

At times it may seem fun to talk about a lame person who has a limp, one who lisps, or struggles to get a word out.

Overlook such defects. Be tolerant.

Never, never put words in others' mouths. Let them have the pleasure of finding the lost word themselves, even if you know the very word they are searching for.

Be civil.

Ways to Be Civil

The bus driver who helps people on board, is civil.

The grocery clerk who carries a heavy package to an elderly customer's car, is being civil.

Look around you for chances to be civil—especially toward those working under you, or trying to sell you something.

Many purchasing agents offices today are air conditioned. There is a pot of coffee and a soft drink machine available.

If the purchasing agent is held up, he is civil enough to come out and explain his delay. That's being civil where it counts most.

*

"Dogs have no prejudice against the poor," reads an Indian proverb.

It is one you should cultivate.

You must never flaunt your wealth before the poor; never brag of your accomplishments; never belittle the efforts of others.

That's a way to become successful in life.

*

Many a good face is hidden under a ragged old hat.

*

Though you whisper about others, your words are thunder in their ears! So be thoughtful of others.

Don't talk even in whispers behind people's backs—for others will then wonder what you say behind *their* backs.

The Story of Lars Eric

Lars Eric Lindblad has built a travel business based on civility. He is a good listener first, a good talker second.

In his New York office next to the Stork Club, he is visited by men and women who want to travel. He is quick to invite them to tell him of *their* desires, *their* daydreams, *their* castles in Spain.

He listens attentively.

He even bends forward to hear every word.

By being civil, he has built a big travel business from "scratch."

The Story of Thomas Cook

Dick Hartley of Thomas Cook & Son is another civil listener. He and Mr. E. O'Connor, the president of the U. S. offices, know the art of being civil even to people who are rude.

Larry Miglierina is a good student of these two men—he, too, has learned the Cook art of being a civil listener, along with Hal Weston of this travel firm.

Never once does any employee break into the verbal daydreams of people who visit the Thomas Cook offices. They listen *first*—then advise *second*.

Thomas Cook himself set the pattern when, as a travel man in England, he saw the handicap of having to sell a traveler many tickets for each phase of a trip across Europe.

He went to the railroads and told them of his idea to sell one ticket good for an entire trip across Europe. They liked the idea—and so began Thomas Cook's firm of travel advisors.

A business built on civility.

*

As Lady Mary Wortley Montague once said: "Civility costs nothing—and buys everything!"

It will buy you the respect of others—their goodwill, and their blessing.

*

The Story of Little Anne

A little girl named Anne Martin one day smiled at Hans Bergen in the Dutch village of Ide. Anne had overlooked

Han's ugliness that prompted other boys and girls to snicker at his repulsiveness.

What happened?

When Hans passed on, he willed Anne $40,000.

The will read: "All the rest of you have frowned or looked away when I passed down the street. But Anne, when I met her one day, gave me a friendly smile, the only one in all my life."

That's a great story; it results from being civil to others.

It's No Great Effort

Courtesy requires no great effort.

But being courteous to others pays off in mental satisfaction.

Manners, I found in my own travels, vary country by country—but courtesy never does.

You may not speak the language, but the common language of all is courtesy—letting others pass through doors before you, picking up packages they have dropped, helping people on trams and across streets.

All these acts put YOU in a pleasant frame of mind.

Never correcting others, never putting them "in line," never looking hard at strangers—all are signs of one born of courtesy. By being civil, it helps you to reach your goal in life.

CHAPTER THOUGHT

If you want to have many friends, learn the art of being civil. It is the oil that makes life less squeaky.

"At the bathing beach which men are gentlemen?"

WHEELERGRAMS TO SUCCESS

Heard from many tongues!

A word is not a bird: once on the wing it can never be caught again.
Don't give nuts to a squirrel when its teeth are no more.
There is no answer, but civility, to a stupid question.
Straddle two horses and you'll fall in the mud.
Don't bother to be born handsome—just be born gracious.
He who rushes at life dies young.
A friendly companion cuts the journey in half.
A hundred friends are not too many—but one enemy is.
If you ride in a man's cart, be prepared to sing his songs.

18

How to use the "kingly feeling"
in making others feel important and
un-cheated of the pleasure of
"being needed"

> *"The worst sin toward our fellow creatures is not*
> *to hate them but to be indifferent to them."*
> —George Bernard Shaw

When an Indianapolis firm went on strike, Bertha didn't join. "How come?" asked her friends, the union, her employers. "I feel needed," she said. "Needed?" "Yes, needed to keep these offices spick and span."

That gave the owner an idea. He'd make the others feel needed, and he did just that. After the strike he showed each helper how his job was "needed." He made the sweeper realize a clean floor was needed to encourage customers; that a clean counter was needed to make customers pleased with the store's appearance.

He went from floor to floor, office to office, helping to make each person feel needed, and you know, that store has yet to have another major strike.

*

When you can give that "kingly feeling" to others, you win them to your side. We all want to be needed. To be king—or at least to have that kingly feeling.

Don't Be a Chronic Check Grabber

I have made it a habit, at times, to let the other person pick up the check in a restaurant. At first blush, it sounds miserly. But when you become a check grabber, you make the other person feel inferior for he likes the opportunity to treat too.

Let the other person have the kingly feeling. Let him pay the check, give a gift, invite you out. For it makes him feel mighty good.

The kingly feeling isn't reserved for kings in real castles, but for kings among all men. Be willing to make a friend by letting him feel needed by you.

Benjamin Franklin flattered a person he wanted to win over by asking for the loan of a book.

That person felt important by Ben's approach. He felt needed and superior because he was the owner of a book that Franklin wanted to read. Yet Franklin's tactic won over a hesitant friend.

Be quick to bolster up the other's ego by making him feel needed.

The Clay Pot Story

One day en route to Toluca, the Friday market place near Mexico City, Senor G. Guajardo Davis, a long-time friend, stopped a Mexican peon and asked, "May I buy one of the pots you are carrying on your head and lighten your load?"

"Not here . . . not here . . ." remarked the Mexican, "but in the market place."

"But here I will pay as much and lighten your burden," said Senor Guajardo Davis, but that was no use. The Mexican replied, "If I sell them to you *here* you will be cheating me."

"Cheating you?" exclaimed the startled Guajardo Davis. "How come?"

"You will be cheating me of the pleasure of talking with you in my little stall at the market place."

This same demonstration was later given me by Jimmy Dubin, the renowned travel agent of Mexico, and after twice seeing this incident I analyzed just why the Mexican would not sell on the highway and lighten his load. This was my reasoning:

The Mexican felt important in his own stall. It was his place of business. It gave him pride—it gave him that kingly feeling. To sell a pot on the highway was next to being an itinerant beggar, so to speak—and the man's pride was hurt. He felt undignified. He felt unimportant.

And that brings up the subject: how to help a man feel kingly.

> *Never, never let a man*
> *do something that causes him*
> *to lose his pride*

When a man's pride is hurt, he will react against you.

Certain jobs seem to be below the Plimsoll mark of a person's pride, and if you put him into that ugly position, he will resent you inwardly.

Yet there always comes a time when a floor must be swept by a secretary; the star salesman must call on "the little customer;" the wife must carry out a garbage can in an emergency; hubby might have to crawl under the house; son might have to take the ugly duckling to the prom—jobs below their pride. Unless handled with tact, the people involved can be hurt immeasurably.

The trick?

It is this: *Do or say something to make that person realize you fully understand the assignment is below his dignity, but the emergency calls for it.*

Get down on your own knees and start brushing, to show the other person you'd do the job. Take the broom and start the sweeping yourself. Tell your salesman, "I would call on the little fellow myself, George, but it is more important I do this. Would you mind this one time making the call yourself? I know it is a small one—*but you'd be helping ME!*"

That's the trick.

"You will be helping ME!"

In that way you make the other person once more feel important. He is HELPING you, obeying your orders; that saves his face and the humble job gets done.

It's Good Leadership

Learn art of leadership.

Be willing, yourself, to do the job—then let the other person realize how much he is helping you.

He'll do the job with pride.

Another leadership technique is to say, "I know it is a small assignment, *but it is right down your alley*. It is something you—*only you*—are skilled in. I hate to trust it to another person. Would you mind doing it this once?"

Of course that person will not refuse. You gave him a chance to save his pride—his face—you made him an important person.

That's a mighty good way to sell yourself to others. It will help you to go places in life through good leadership, with a knowledge of how to inspire people to do things for you willingly.

Make People Feel Responsible

Many an advice-to-the-love-lorn columnist has received a letter saying: "My husband is a good provider. He gives me all I want, except one thing; he feels I can't do things. He never lets me do anything *for myself!*"

The wife is suffering from loss of pride, loss of confidence. With a husband who wants to do everything himself, the wife is robbed of the thrill of doing things on her own.

It is often wise, therefore, to give "assignments" to others. If that person feels he is "responsible" for certain things, he responds more energetically. He has a task to do. He goes to it.

It gives him the kingly feeling.

Three More Magic Words

There are three other magic words in getting along with others, which are: *"I need you."*

Whenever you say "I need you" to someone, you get their immediate and undivided attention. They are on your side at once.

One tactic is to ask others to do simple things for you, but things they might be proud of, or skilled in. "Will you help me fix my lawnmower?" says the neighbor, and gets action at once if he adds, "I need your advice."

"I need you" are three words useful for successful relations with others.

Ask small favors of workers. They gladly respond. One boss I know often stops a worker, fumbles his change, then asks the worker, "Charlie, have you a dime for a coke? I'm all out of money."

Charlie is proud to give the boss a ten cent piece! Proud

to have the chief owe Charlie a dime.

Small, yes—but it made Charlie feel good.

But Don't Over-do It

Ben Franklin put it this way: "He that hath once done you a kindness will be more ready to do you another, than he whom you yourself have obliged."

To lose friends, says a philosopher, at once loan them money. Then they will avoid meeting you forever.

WARNING: Don't become a bum! That is, don't over-do the asking. Once, twice may be fine in getting money for a coke, in borrowing a cigarette, in asking the aid of a friend to fix a lawnmower. Just don't become a bummer. Know when to stop the stunt.

"It is as blessed to receive as to give," say the Oriental philosophers.

Be a Giver Yourself

Yet you can gain love and friendships by being a good giver yourself, expecting nothing in return.

Buddha puts it in this fine language:

The charitable man is loved by all; his friendship is prized highly; in death his heart is at rest and full of joy, for he suffers not from repentance; he receives the open flower of his reward and the fruit that ripens from it. Hard it is to understand: by giving away food, we get more strength; by bestowing clothing on others, we gain more beauty; by donating abodes of purity and truth, we acquire great treasures.

Therefore, to win staunch and lasting friendships, be alert to ask for small favors; hurried to say, "I need you." But be willing to give back in return your love and respect, your food and clothing. But expect nothing in return but friendship.

Let a person "do it himself." It builds his ego and pride in himself for being "wanted." Make people around you feel "wanted," and they will respond in kind.

Buddha says, "There is a proper time and a proper mode in charity; just as the vigorous warrior goes to battle, so is the man who is able to give . . . he gives with reverence, and banishes all hatred, envy and anger."

The man who makes good use of his wealth is rightly said to possess a great treasure; but the miser who hoards up his riches will have no profit.

Buddha further says in his writings, "Charity is rich in returns; charity is the greatest wealth, for though it scatters, it brings no repentance."

For those of you not rich in money may still be rich in the wealth within you—your thoughts.

You can give your thoughts to others—and still retain them for yourself. You can pass thoughts on to others—scattering your innermost wealth, passing it on to others just as the rich man passes out gold.

Learn the art of passing along your thoughts to others, making them richer. Build your castle with blocks of friendship, not money. When you do give, give wisely—and expect no material returns, just some fleeting moments of thankfulness.

To share the wealth of your thoughts with others gives them a treasure that cannot be foolishly spent or wasted. The recipient becomes a part of your thinking, your thoughts—and he is better for it.

"Gifts are great, the founding of temples is meritorious, meditations and religious exercises pacify the heart, comprehension of truth leads to Nirvana—but greater than all is loving kindness."—Buddha

How Old Is The Smile?

The editors of *Vogue* magazine recently asked the question, "How old is the smile?"

This set me to thinking—for I have noted the smile seemed unknown in the days of the cavemen, perhaps because they were too busy fighting the elements (and each other), to smile.

But today we often smile. Firms have "smile days" and "smile contests," for the smile is a modern way to win others to our thinking, and to make firm friends.

Of interest in the *Vogue* story was the illustration of a statue of a Mexican clay figure of about 700 A.D. The clay face was all smiles, of the same kind so familiar to us today. This indicates that the smile does have a history as a way of expressing satisfaction among friends.

How old is the smile?

We may never know.

But we do know that it is a great tool and tactic today to encourage people like us, and help us achieve our goals.

19

The art of good conversation
is to let the other fellow
do the talking about himself!

"He who would be too clever makes a fool of himself."

Disraeli learned the art of encouraging the other person to do the talking, and progressed from an ordinary politician to a great statesman and prime minister.

His presence was always in great demand by society. Why? Because Disraeli had learned one secret—*inspire the other person to talk about—himself.*

You can't learn when your mouth is open.

That's the philosophy of another "great talker," Jack Frazier, who had the idea he could make better loud speakers than anyone else in hi-fi, and did it.

How?

"Not by talking," said Frazier, "but by listening. I would egg-on hi-fi fans to talk about what they liked and what they found lacking in hi-fi speakers. By listening I learned what was needed—what was wanted—what people would pay money to buy, and I built just such a speaker."

Jack's "listen first, talk second" program has developed into a great electronics business, with headquarters in Dallas. His hi-fi speakers are all over the world. They do the talking for Jack, the "silent listener."

Dwight Morrow Listened Well

Dwight Morrow, as the story was told to me in Mexico, won the respect of President Calles not by doing the talking, but by listening.

Calles had expected another "great glib talker from the U. S." to overwhelm him with talk about the U. S., but Morrow fooled Calles. They had breakfast, but after cigars were lighted, and Calles sat back to be "sold a bill of U. S. goods," Morrow said, *"Please tell me about Mexico!"*

The Parental Approach

Latin Americans like the parental approach.

They like to talk about their families first upon meeting, and to pass pictures of the children around—then talk business.

It is very improper to rush into a Latin American business office and say, "To save time, let's get down to business."

"Time is of no essence," the Latin American will tell you. "First tell me about yourself. Are you married? How many children?"

That to him is more important than business—to win over this man from below the border (or in your very home city), use this same sort of parental approach. Get the other person to talk first—*about himself.*

Listeners Have the Advantage

There is an old-world adage that says: "If I listen I have the advantage; if I speak others have it."

Or as Jack Frazier puts it, "A fish dies by an open mouth!"

When you see an important person in business or social life, you'll see a great listener.

Human nature is such that we all want:

To *impress* others how smart we are.
To feel *important.*
To feel *needed* and wanted by others.
To have people *respect* our ideas.
To be "somebody."

One important way to capitalize on these instincts in people to win them over and to gain their respect is to let them do the talking—about themselves.

Be a good listener.

Bend forward, *mentally.*

*

There is an old saying: "When the mind becomes large, the speech becomes little."

*

The more you know—often the less you should talk.

People do become gabby to hide a lack of something, perhaps education or ability, a weakness that they hope glib conversation will cover up. Beware of the man who rattles at the mouth!

Respect the silent one. For still water does run deep.

The Trick of Wordly Women

Carole Lombard won Clark Gable with a simple tactic: "I was the best audience he ever had."

Worldly women, women of palaces and kingdoms, won their position by being first a good listener—a fine audience for some prince or potential husband who was hungry for attention.

Worldly women know this. So should humble Main Street wives in your own home town; all men love attention.

Often a woman, loaded with jewels and cars, is the wonder of her friends. "How did you manage it?" they ask, and of course the answer usually is, "They give rapt attention to their men."

This is a knack that clever women acquire instinctively. It's a technique you can use in winning your man—and holding him.

It is said of Peggy Hopkins Joyce, the much admired and popular woman of a few years back, "When she entered a room she glanced at all the men, but then *concentrated* on the one at hand."

She gave him her fullest attention, and it paid off in other dates with envious men.

Remember: the rich woman was first a good audience.

"The wise man has long ears."

WHY WORRY?

Does this headline look familiar, like something out of this morning's newspaper?

PREDICT EARLY WAR WITH RUSSIA

Well, don't worry. It was the headline in the New York Sun on January 12, 1900.

The same paper ran another headline:

BOERS BELIEVED TO HAVE LOST 2,000

And still another read:

STUDENT'S PRANK STOPS CONCERT AT HARVARD

You see headlines remain the same year after year—so why worry?

20

Word magic

"Don't use oil paper to wrap up fire!"

I went to see Leo Calhoun recently to have my Newcomb tape recorder put in order.

I said, "I'd like to have it fixed, Leo."

Leo has had years of experience in choosing the right words to make people appreciate his services, and "fixing" wasn't one of his words. "I *adjust* sets—I *service* them," he told me. "I don't fix 'em."

I caught on.

I then asked Leo, "Give me some other examples of good words that make friends of people. I realize that repairmen these days are having trouble with the public who feel that they are always being gypped, cheated, or otherwise taken advantage of by repairmen."

Leo went on: "One day I told a woman I had merely *bent* a part in her machine to fix it, and she nearly went into a rage: '*Bent* a part in my machine?' she shouted, 'How horrible!' "

"Now I tell people I have *adjusted* their *instrument*."

I liked Leo Calhoun's thinking of how a service man can build friendships and business with proper word-magic.

Choose Words Wisely

I can remember going into an old-time auto agency and, as the seller talked to me about his shiny new car, I saw a sign over it blinking on and off: REPAIR DEPT.

That always caused me to wonder.

Nowadays it is the SERVICE or the MAINTENANCE DEPT. Better word magic.

So I begged Leo and he went on:

"I am not a hi-fi *repairman*. No sir, I can't command respect with that word. I am an *electronic service man*. I'm a *technical man* that has been factory trained, not a fixer-upper."

I liked Leo's choice of words. He had a sensitive understanding of people and how to win them over to his point of view by gaining their admiration and respect. Both are qualities which anyone dealing with people must have to exist in business today.

The Story of Bill Lear

I ran into another advocate of word magic—dynamic Bill Lear, founder and Chairman of the Board of one of America's biggest producers of aircraft instruments. He found success the hard way, the "insecure way."

"Insecure way?" you ask, and Lear will tell you:

"Develop a little *insecurity*. If you have a sound idea for a business or a new product, why not borrow money? I'm paying $200 a day interest alone on the money I've borrowed. The responsibility of paying it off makes me work that much harder."

The choice of the off-beat word "insecurity" is real word-magic. It is usually a word that people fear, yet Lear, running a multi-million dollar business he built from scratch, should know the value of insecurity in prodding oneself higher up the ladder of success.

Lear's Three Rules

Want some more inside dope from this man Lear?

1. *Work an extra hour each day.* Sure it sounds trite, but all success mottos are trite.
2. *Don't forget to use common sense.* Lear claims there are thousands of people with ideas that look terrific on paper, but the public refuses to accept them. "Common sense is foresight," says Lear.
3. *Don't be lazy.* Lear points to the downfall of Rome, China, Egypt and other empires that fell apart when people got lazy and slacked off.

These mottos are as old-fashioned as sulphur and molasses, but they still work today. Ask any successful man and he will say "Lear is right."

There is no fancy language in these mottos—but lots of magic!

Clarence Dunning's Philosophy

Clarence Dunning uses word magic in his insurance business.

He doesn't sell *death* insurance, but *living* insurance.

It is LIVING INSURANCE that people want, he says, not something with the word "death" in it.

I can see Dunning's thinking, too, and I like it.

Weigh Words Well

"Words should be weighed, not counted," says an ancient merchant in Damascus, the oldest city of trade and commerce. As I went through the bazaars of that city, I saw word-magic all around me.

Each seller painted word-pictures of what he sells. "These are Arabian worry-beads," said one seller. "You fiddle with them to relieve your tension."

So I bought a pair to fiddle with.

"It took 3 women 6 months to hand-weave this material," said another seller, and my wife purchased a Damascus table cloth.

The American dealer might say (if he said anything at all to the customer), "This table cloth looks swell, doesn't it? And will last through many washings."

Women buy table cloths to impress their friends, not the laundry man.

So it goes—and so must you. Look around for magic words to put yourself across with others.

"You look good *today*," is a near insult to some people, who wonder, "How'd I look *yesterday?*"

That's not good word-magic.

"This TV set has transistors now," means little to people. What they buy is the picture, not the means of getting the picture.

The Old Testament puts it this way: "How forcible are right words."

Be Friendly—Not Frank

"Don't tell your friends their social faults: they will cure the faults and never forgive you."

That's a proverb for all of us to practice.

We are too quick to let words fly that put the other person in his place, or that criticize him.

That's not practicing good word-magic!

Don't be frank with people; instead be friendly!

Friendly people overlook faults of others, and others overlook their faults—and the whole world is happier.

Don't Make Demands

Change, "What have I got coming?" to "What can I offer you?"

The seller, business executive, husband, wife, neighbor— all can profit by this doctrine of word-magic.

When we want a raise we tell the boss what *we* can do to warrant the raise—not what *he* has to do.

You may have it coming—but don't express it that way.

The fellow who sits back and says, "The world owes me a living" will never collect. Demanding things is poor psychology. Offering things gets things in return.

This is "intelligent selfishness"—to offer help to others, for then in return they will offer to help you.

As Aristotle asks: "Should a man love himself most, or someone else?" His answer: ". . . a bad man seems to do everything for his own sake."

Unless workers see what is in it for them, unions have trouble getting their workers to strike. Good business firms today emphasize to the workers the benefits they are getting, not those the stockholders will receive.

That's sound word-magic.

It is stupid to be selfish.
It is better to be selfishly unselfish!
This is to help yourself by helping others.

*

In giving the world the electric light, Edison brought himself fame—just as Ford, Thomas J. Watson, Carnegie and Schwab did in their field.

When you give something to the world, you automatically get something in return.

*

Good word-magic is to let the other fellow argue your own case for you.

Many an "assistant president" has brought ideas to the President, letting him absorb them to the point the President thinks of them as his own ideas, and will argue the case for their adoption more forcibly.

The method is to make the other person thirsty for what you have; then he will want to drink.

Four Good Tips to Use

Here is good word magic in handling people:

1. "As you said sometime ago . . ."
2. "I agree with you, but . . ."
3. "Last time you said . . ."
4. "I see your point, and suggest . . ."

These bits of word-magic inflate the other's ego, and he will argue your case for you—as if they were his own ideas.

Putting ideas and words into someone else's mouth isn't always an easy task, but with word-magic you can do it. It requires tact and diplomacy of the kind Colonel House always used with President Wilson, quietly presenting ideas to Wilson as the President's own.

I have seen Tom Hickey, of the Hickey-Freeman Clothing Company, suggest style ideas to the salesmen of stores he visits. He doesn't say, "These are our designers' ideas. You will use them." Instead he offers several alternates to the sellers and asks, "Which of these styles do you feel will sell best in your store?"

He is using our sales point No. 4: "Don't Ask If—Ask Which."

It gives a person a choice between something and something, never between something and nothing. It works magically.

Four More Good Word-Handles

Discuss—don't argue.

That's real word-magic.

Here are four more good "word handles" to use.

1. "I always thought so myself, until I . . ."
2. "I used to think the same thing, then one day . . ."
3. "You have really thought it out. Have you also thought about . . . ?"
4. "I like your thinking. What is your opinion about . . . ?"

You won't offend people with this language. You'll excite their interest and gain their respect.

Discuss—don't argue.

Patrick Henry didn't tell congress what to do: he placed the choice before them by saying, "Give me liberty or give me death!"

That was reverse selling de luxe!

Don't tell 'em—ask 'em.

Abe Lincoln often argued the other person's side: this robbed them of the opportunity to state their own case.

Test this logic. Its reaction on others is terrific.

"I see your side clearly. I understand it thoroughly. You are so right in many things. But then one day I saw my side. I saw how it differed somewhat from yours, and I would like your opinion of my side."

How much further you can get from this word-magic than to contradict, outright, the other person's thinking . . . insulting his ideas . . . making him angry with you . . . closing the door?

Don't tell 'em—ask 'em.

Used Back in Rome

Brutus had a knack of bringing up subjects cleverly, not in a demanding manner. Remember his lines?

"Had you rather Caesar were living, and die all slaves, than that Caesar were dead, to live all free men?"

It's a great example of presenting a case for discussion, by the use of our point No. 4: "Don't Ask If—Ask Which."

Two Sides to the Axe

The woodsman always uses both sides of the axe.

How far would Brutus have gotten if he had come out bluntly and said, "Yes, I killed Caesar—so what?"

How far would Leo Calhoun get if he continued to "bend" the "machines" of his customers'?

How far would Clarence Talley get if he sold "foreign jobs," instead of imports?

CHAPTER THOUGHT

Forced feeding won't make people swallow what you have to offer them, so never argue—only discuss. Don't tell people— ask them. Toss away your whiskers, and substitute word-magic.

"The highest art is the art of concealing bad thoughts."

WHICH OF THESE PHOBIAS DO YOU HAVE?

So you think you have a phobia?

Too often people fear they have a phobia, and the fear holds them back in life.

Maybe when you see this Master List of Phobias, you'll feel your phobia is nothing to fear after all.

PHOBIA LIST

Here are a few of the many phobias of modern Americans:

Acousticophobia—fear of sounds.
Acrophobia—fear of heights.
Aerophobia—fear of air.
Agoraphobia—fear of wide-open spaces.
Algophobia—fear of pain.
Autophobia—fear of being alone.
Cainotophobia—fear of a new environment.
Claustrophobia—fear of enclosed spaces.
Cynophobia—fear of dogs or rabies.
Erythrophobia— fear of red or blushing.
Gamophobia—fear of marriage.
Hedonophobia—fear of pleasure.
Nosophobia—fear of disease.
Nyctophobia—fear of darkness.
Panophobia—fear of some indefinite evil.
Pantophobia—fear of everything.
Ponophobia—fear of work.
Sitophobia—fear of eating.
Xenophobia—fear of strangers.

21

A tactic used by reporters
to open up a person and make him really
"see" and "hear" you

"The best horse cannot wear two saddles."

The tactic is simple; one I often used myself, instinctively, when I was selling space for Hearst newspapers.

It is a matter of getting people to talk about something they are proud of, *but not an expert in doing.*

To ask a banker's advice on banking might make him feel you are merely flattering him for the purpose of obtaining a good loan; but to ask the banker his advice on his hobby, fishing for flounder in the Sound, will prompt him to open up.

To get people to talk freely, tactfully invite them to answer a question on something they aren't necessarily good in, but enjoy doing.

How I Won Wilbur May

One time I asked Wilbur May, head of the May Company department stores, "Where did you learn to fly an airplane?"

He opened up.

He warmed up.

In fact, I spent that week-end with him and his wife in Atlantic City so that he could show me his ability as an airplane pilot. This, of course, was a long time ago, before "family planes" were as common as they are today.

If I had asked Wilbur May, who at the time managed the Baltimore store, about merchandising, buying, or retailing, he'd have been bored. That was his work. Flying an airplane was his side-line.

Needless to say, Wilbur May placed more advertisements with us that year than were given to our mighty competitor, the *Baltimore News*.

When the figures came out for comparison, and it was known I had secured the greater share of this business for the first time in Baltimore newspaper history, my boss, Erwin Huber, had me stand up in front of the sales staff, and invited me to "Tell the boys how you got the business."

I stood up. I wobbled a bit. Then said, "I asked him how he learned to fly an airplane."

I sat down.

My boss mentally sat down.

I guess I wasn't very enlightening. Erwin didn't know my ungrammatical rule:

Everybody likes praise on something he's not good in.

*

A trick to win friendships is to give people authority— small as it may seem.

This is a second good tactic to use to get ahead in life.

It is the art of delegating authority where it counts most.

I'm Given "Authority"

I can remember Erwin Huber calling me in the day after our sales conference—at which I had so poorly explained how I sold Wilbur May.

"Elmer, you are in charge of the downtown department stores," he told me.

I puffed to the sky. That WAS authority!

Erwin Huber knew it was—knew it would inspire me to extra effort. I really went to town, and tried more than ever to use intelligent sales tactics winning others over.

Now, years later, I see the value of giving authority to others.

I did so just the other day in my own home. "Emma," I said to our maid, "you do such a good job with flowers, I'm putting you in charge of my favorite garden." Her eyes popped out—not for the fun of working in the garden, nor the extra work it entailed, but the fact that "the boss man" had given her authority.

She was in charge of the garden. She! Not Pat, our yard boy. But Emma!

Be a Good Casting Director

One way to handle this tactic is to be a good casting director with people. Do this by knowing which person to make the hero, which the heroine, which the banker, doctor, lawyer.

Have confidence in knowing the other person will react as you hope he will. It forces him to "live up" to your expectations and to maintain his reputation.

People, however, can form the wrong images of you.

This is harmful. You may be known as the shy guy, the quiet and backward one—the person "who won't stand on his own opinions." These are images that won't help you get across with others. If you are classed as the shy guy, make this your motto: DON'T LIE DOWN.

People love to walk on soft rugs—and on people who are softees. If you lie down in life, soon others will tramp over you as they use you to gain their own ends. This is a poor position to be in. Assert yourself.

Don't Be Last in Line

Some people never get anywhere in life. They are the last in line, sit in the back seat, never seem to be able to "crash" a restaurant. Yet others always have tickets for this, seats for that. They aren't rudely aggressive, but they use tact plus determination to get places in life.

One trick is to watch the "attitude" of people. A man or woman walks regally into a restaurant, and actually "commands" attention—and what is more important, gets it.

Then the shy guy creeps into the place. No wonder he isn't able to impress the management enough to get a good table. He's the corner-seat diner!

Your attitude—your manners—your way of walking, talking and standing—gives them a mental picture of your personality. It tells them if you are a person who will insist on attention.

Tip: *don't lie down.*

Let *everybody* think you are *somebody*.

Try It in the Home

If you want fun in life, do become a good casting director.

Give assignments—give authority—where it will work for both you and the other person.

Don't ask the wife to make your business calls; let her be in "charge of the kitchen," or whatever assignment you feel will elevate her ego and give her prestige and attention.

Tell son Wilbur, "You are in charge of raking leaves this fall. Mary, daughter, you are in charge of the vacuum cleaner brigade."

This is a better tactic than to give an order and demand obedience.

Make someone a captain, another a lieutenant—make another a general, and you will go places in life.

Civic clubs and other groups do this to raise funds. Each will divide and take sides, issuing authority. "You are General in charge of the Black Group, and you, Bill, are General in charge of the Red Group. The losers eat crow. The winners eat turkey."

One Tip in Fund Raising That Will
Raise a Million Dollars!

I was asked once by several fund-raising groups, such as the Red Cross, for a single sentence to use in both door-to-door and telephone solicitation that would win a person's support in a hurry.

It would not be tactful to tell you where the idea originated, but it worked wonders.

It was not the usual, "Will you give to my charity this year?" for that had two answers: Yes or No.

The suggestion was: "How GENEROUS will you be this year?"

What person, so addressed, would say, "No, I'm not going to be generous this year."

The person was whizzled—he was sizzled with the 4th Wheelerpoint I so often mention (as has *Reader's Digest, Fortune,* the *New Yorker*), where the prospective donor was told, "Last year you gave $50. Which can you afford to give this year: $100 *or* $150?"

The choice between $100 and $150 was often too steep. The person would usually split the difference, often saying, "Well, $100 is about what I feel I can afford this year."

The tactic: Give the other person a chance to be GENEROUS!

*

Always assume the best intentions in a person. Then you may succeed in arousing them to do their best.

*

"You can't fool all of the people all of the time—but somebody is always trying."

That's another proverb—one you should avoid to get ahead in the business world.

Sure you can "trick" your son into doing something one time, but don't try it the second time.

You can trick a worker once to stay overtime, but the trick may boomerang the second time.

Don't take people for fools!

People Are Really Smart

"No one has a good market for bad goods."

That's a mighty solid business doctrine, one for you to practice that will gain the confidence of others—that confidence so necessary to make sales in the business world.

One firm recently put out a car that had new-type brakes that proved faulty. What did they do? They issued orders to all their dealers: "Replace the brakes at once—and at no charge."

This won new confidence in that firm's products.

You will buy a watch off a street corner tout just once, for usually you find it is worthless.

Yet, in the airports of Zurich, Geneva—anywhere in

Switzerland—you can feel safe in buying the most expensive watch, for the manufacturers' association and the Swiss government is behind these little "shops" in airports.

At what airport in the U. S. would you have such confidence? To buy a souvenir, perhaps—but a $1,000 Patek Phillip watch? Hardly!

Confidence is something to establish quickly with the people you plan to do business with and to assure you of good relations over the long pull.

And, as with the car maker, if you do suddenly find that what you have sold doesn't live up to your reputation, be quick—before the purchaser asks you—to replace, repair, or otherwise correct the error.

Don't try to fool people. They are *smarter* than you think!

Pick Your Right "Face"

You can't wear two faces in dealing with people.

Determine which "face" you want to sell to others: reliability, honesty, friendliness, determination, frankness—whatever face you feel fits your personality, then wear it.

But don't suddenly show up with another face.

Like the horse, you can't wear two saddles—one for one customer, one for another—one for one friend, another for the other.

Even politicians are finding this out.

A good Santa Claus never wears a false face.

Watch Your First Ten Words

Watch, too, the first words you use to put yourself across with others, or to make a sale.

Your first ten words, when meeting others, are more important than your next 10,000.

In fact, if the first ten words aren't the right ones, you won't have a chance to use the next 10,000.

As the Oriental salesman puts it, "If the first words fail . . . 10,000 will not then avail!"

The Story of Russ Mamminga

"Learning is a treasure no thief can touch."

If you want to get along in life, socially or businesswise, do as Russ Mamminga does. He represents the famed Hathaway shirt firm, and when I met his many friends around the country, I asked them what made Russ a success. The answer was always, "He knows shirts!"

He has become an expert on shirts, not only those of his own firm, but those of his competitors, and, as his dealers say, "When Russ talks, you listen."

I asked, "Why do you listen?"

"Because," they told me, "he is a treasure-house of information. He gives us facts that other sellers don't give. They merely sell us—Russ educates us in shirting materials, manufacturing processes, styling and so forth. He is loaded with information."

And that is a mighty good way to make progress—be "loaded with information." Have a good background in whatever you do. Be "up" on golf, if that is your hobby; be "up" on any subject that you speak on, be that treasure-house of information.

There is no need to be a shy guy in life if you are "loaded" with knowledge, for people will flock around to seek information. "Always see Charlie," they say, "if you really want to know about that subject."

"Learning is weightless . . . a treasure you always carry easily."—Chinese Proverb

A Big Secret in Applying Your Word Power!

Lastly, if you want to sell yourself to others, talk in "living color."

Paint word pictures. Use Technicolor words.

Edison described electricity by saying it was like a dachshund, ". . . when you pull the tail in Edinburgh he would bark in London."

Even I can now understand electricity!

One picture like this does replace a thousand words.

Many a preacher has taught his philosophy through parables, for they are "living color."

The good speaker frequently uses "for instance" and "for example" in getting his point across. Always be quick to double your word-power by saying, "Let me give you an example."

Use the words "see," "feel," "touch," "smell," "hold," in conversing with people, and watch their interest grow in what you are saying to them. Dr. Russell Conwell in his famed lecture, "Acres of Diamonds," had the knack of choosing colorful words. He showed people how to find success "in your own backyard."

Napoleon said, "People will point you out as having been with the army in Italy." This bolstered the morale of the men who visualized the great acclaim they'd get back home from family and friends.

Hitler painted visions of glory and power for the masses, just as Castro, Peron and others have done to inspire people to follow their leadership, false as it may have been. Khrushchev told us, "I will bury you." A horrible thought—but a powerful word picture.

Speak in "Living Color"

If you will make use of word pictures in living color to promote good, you will find yourself a leader among men.

Don't talk in plain black and white. Color is the thing today.

Use simple language. Will Rogers put it this way, "I like words but I don't like strange ones." He knew that strange language might highlight a college education, but there is a chance the words may be misunderstood.

Say something simple.

Avoid jawbreakers!

Use picture words—in color.

And when in doubt, use parables—many "for instances" and innumerable "for examples." Use a blackboard when needed; draw pictures when they will help the other person see what you see. Shakespeare said, "Suit the action to the word, the word to the action."

Get excited—and others will get excited.

Talk sluggishly with word whiskers, and others will mentally fall asleep in front of you, if they don't actually walk away. Be colorful. Talk colorfully.

CHAPTER THOUGHT

The more you concentrate on what you say, the deeper your words will burn into the minds of the listeners. For words like the sunshine, must be concentrated to be really felt.

RED SKELTON'S FRIEND-MAKER

When Red Skelton leaves you he never says, "Good luck."
No sir!
He's an inveterate believer luck has little to do with your success, so his parting line is often, *"Continued Success!"*

22

The importance of being trivial
and using "small talk" in getting
yourself over with others

"The little learned man is useful to the state—
what use the great big blockheads?"—Buddha

"I like to sit at this Round Table," said Bill Painter to
John Erhard, who replied, "Yes, it is relaxing to sit here."

I then asked these two why they liked the Round Table,
located in the Dallas Athletic Club, where a few select men
gather each day. "Is it because you meet other important
business men?" I asked, "Or is it because you hear valuable
discussions of help in your business?"

As one man both shook their heads and replied, "No—it is
because of *trivial* conversation."

This threw me for a moment, and then I saw what they
meant.

"I get enough business talk in my office," said Erhard,
"and it is a pleasure just to hear small talk and talk small
talk. It relaxes me."

Painter nodded in approval.

A few days later I was at another famous Round Table, the one headed by Ben Bodne and Sidney Colby in the Algonquin Hotel in New York City, where such men as Robert Benchley and others gathered. I sat back to listen to what these gentlemen talked about—again it was trivial subjects.

Again, men were attracted by the opportunity to engage in small talk.

There were writers, lawyers, and insurance executives such as Elmer Letterman, none of whom talked "shop"—or inquired into the others' business affairs except on rare occasions. Again the men relaxed for an hour or so of trivia.

The Importance of Trivia

I realized then the importance of trivia, of talking on minor subjects—but seldom about shop.

To be sure, they gave their ideas on how to run the government, what they'd do if they were in the State Department, how they'd react to various world events—but this was not shop talk. Just conversation.

I saw at once the importance of making friends with small talk, and I began to practice it myself at home, at social gatherings, as well as at the two Round Tables. I saw busy people giving me complete attention, anxious to share their ideas on small matters that needed no solution, just pleasant comment.

I now recognize the importance of trivia to help others relax with you,—knowing that they will not be harassed by shop talk, sold some insurance, or become a prospect for some salesman's product.

It is a strategy we all can use to hold on to old friendships —and make new ones.

The Errors of Joke Telling

Telling amusing and funny stories is part of small talk among friends, and this brings up another art: that of how to tell the jokes.

The error of joke tellers too often is:

1. Telling too long stories.
2. Personalizing them on others around.
3. Not giving others a chance to tell their jokes.
4. Making others feel small.

The joke teller who goes on and on with a long story soon loses the interest (and respect) of others. He must learn to pull his yarns tightly together, and come to the point in a hurry. Then he holds the attention of his friends who will welcome his next story.

When a joke is about a personality in the group, that person feels inferior. He may smile—but it is a weak smile. So the trick is never, *never* make anyone present bear the brunt of any story.

Another great error is to dominate a conversation. Someone tells a story. Others hardly laugh at it before you pound on with your joke. This makes the other teller peeved at you. He wanted the full response of all, yet you robbed him of that pleasure. Let a good long laugh come between jokes.

Then you yourself will have the fullest attention for your stories.

Some jokes make people feel embarrassed. Jokes about religion, for example, are not good psychology. Avoid talk about widows when a widow is present, or a story about a tongue-tied person when someone present has the impediment. This is not good Emily Post or Sizzlemanship.

It is not good sense to tell saloon stories outside of saloons, or a salesman's hard-fisted yarn to a group at the Friday

Afternoon Women's Club. You must fit the joke to the occasion, not the occasion to your joke.

Never offend others.

One weakness of jokesters is to fail to fit the joke to the affair with proper timing. To stand up before a group and start off with a Pat and Mike joke that has absolutely no bearing on your speech, isn't promoting the speech very well. Jokes must tie into your speech and fit the content of your talk—never dragged in by the ears just for the joke's sake.

Jack Benny had the right philosophy of telling jokes. They were at his own expense—not others. His jokes about being a tightwad were funny because they were about himself.

So practice this trick: make yourself the humorous butt of the story, not those around you.

*

We laugh only at what makes us feel superior.

*

When a person slips on a banana peel, it makes you laugh, unfortunately, because it makes you feel superior.

Thackeray once said: "Good humor is one of the best articles of dress one can wear in society."

Often tension can be broken by a joke. Politicians realize this. That is why they struggle to ease the tension, and gain attention with a funny story—and this is one time it can be on the other person, the opponent.

Don't Deflate People

To make others the hero is a philosophy of Zenn Kaufman, a student and counselor of methods in winning over others by showmanship. He claims we all want to be the hero of any story, any sale, any joke.

Bruce Barton says, "You can't keep men from getting on well together once they have laughed at some funny stories."

Will Rogers said, "The secret of telling a joke is to tell the right joke at the right place at the right time."

How true this is, for the Irish joke has its place as do Jewish jokes—but in the wrong place they can easily upset people, and make them sad sacks in the eyes of the other listeners. That's not the best way to make lasting friendships.

Don't hog the show. How true that advice is when telling jokes. It is not good to pull a lengthy list of joke after joke out of your pile—but rather to leave people thirsty and hungry for more. Proper timing is valuable. Time your joke so it gets full attention. Never interrupt a conversation just to tell a joke that came suddenly to your mind. And never indicate to other story tellers, wife-fashion, that you've heard their joke. Give them your fullest attention. Keep their respect by laughing at their stories and they will then laugh at yours.

Indicating by side remarks, or smiles on your face, that you've heard the story before doesn't brand you as an egg-head, but as a blockhead.

Don't steal the other person's fun.

*

Often it isn't the joke that is funny, but the person's art in telling it. So if you've heard the joke itself, listen to this person's way of telling it. You may learn something new about the story.

Condense, Condense, Condense

Make 'em short.

Only Scheherazade could tell the story night after night, but that was to save her head.

You'd lose your head quickly if you rambled on.

Never apologize for your story, by saying such trite things as, "If you've heard this before, stop me." Tell it. Tell it fast. Make it short.

Should Snuff Boxes Sneeze?

While some will say, "A snuffbox has no right to sneeze, nor a jokester to laugh at his own jokes," I disagree with them. Laughter is contagious, and you often provoke mirth by laughing at your own stories.

"He really enjoys them," they'll say.

But of course if you laugh too loudly, well that's another thing. The buffoon who thinks he is a great teller of yarns and who laughs unnecessarily at them, perhaps is as bad as a snuffbox that sneezes.

Some story tellers tell jokes with a poker face, such as Joey Bishop. Others laugh like Ed Wynn. Whatever is your own style, use it. Then you are doing something naturally.

Save Situations With Jokes

When you can tell a joke to save a face, or a situation, do so. Jokes can disarm many people. Dorothy Dix says a joke or a jest is "the greatest defense against mashers!"

But if joke-telling is not your talent, then be a good audience. You can win as many friends laughing at others' jokes as in telling your own.

Remember: a good listener is worth two jokesters.

Three Important "Don'ts"

The art of small conversation is necessary in today's tense business and social life.

Be quick to get the other person talking on some small subject, to oil him up—to make him forget his business or home woes. He will relax and enjoy your companionship.

1. Don't become erudite.
2. Don't be a blockhead.
3. Don't be an egg-head.

Be a normal guy who enjoys, at these off-moments, some small talk.

It can be on the other person's hobby, for example, or about something in today's newspaper. But keep it off the serious side. That's for the office or the meeting room, not the luncheon Round Table or the coffee klatsch.

Coffee breaks are for relaxing. Not for serious discussions.

Americans often bring their troubles to the dinner table. That's bad for digestion . . . or making friends. In other parts of the world men sit down to small talk, trivia. They want to figuratively put their feet up on the table, and smoke and enjoy those moments of pleasant association with one another, not to swap business ideas or plans.

Leave the memo pad on the work desk!

The Jumping Bean Moral

I often tell Senor Guajardo Davis' story about the American buyer who said, "I won't buy jumping beans from you, senor. I don't like your face."

The seller didn't get annoyed. Instead he made a joke and replied, "I can't do anything about my face, senor, but I know one thing—*my jumping beans really jump!*"

And when Uncle Joe Cannon, longtime Speaker of the House, was heckled by his opponent about having oats in his pockets like a farmhand, he replied: "Not only do I have oats in my pockets but hayseed in my hair!"

To avoid a serious moment when her husband walked out on a speaker who then got riled, the woman jumped to her feet and said, "You will have to excuse my husband. He walks in his sleep!"

The resultant laughter eased the tension.

Learn the art of being trivial. Use the power of small talk.

Don't be afraid to ease the tension with a funny yarn, especially if it is on yourself.

Make 'em want more!

"Two good talkers are never worth one good listener."

KEEP YOUR CHIN HIGH

Keeping your chin high as you walk down the street of life, gives you a psychological "lift."

It makes you feel stronger, better, and very important.

It has an effect, too, on others. That is why cheer leaders lift their chins high; why the Marine Corps makes its men wear hats low over their forehead, forcing them to keep their chin high to see.

You will "see" that life is better if your chin is always held high.

Try this today. Note how much better you feel. Note the tonic-like effect it has on you—and on others you meet.

Always keep your chin high in life!

23

Zen is the philosophy
the Chinese used centuries ago
to teach man the fallacy of
pressing too hard to win

"From the Old we learn the New."

While Zen goes back centuries, it is still serviceable today.

It is new to the western world, where we are suddenly asking, "What is Zen?"

Zen, a subject that so many are discussing today in America, is an outgrowth of Buddhism. Zen was brought to China and is now also the philosophy and practice of many Japanese. European thought on the matter is also being heard in America. Even Jack Paar talks about Zen on his midnight show, so you see how popular it is becoming.

But to tell you exactly and precisely what Zen is becomes almost impossible.

What Is Zen?

It sounds silly to say Zen is hard to comprehend.

But teachers for centuries have tried to explain Zen, and

have concluded it "cannot be grasped by the intellect but gained only through your intuitive powers." It is nothing you can put your fingers on, like the elusive airs and manners of a well trained old world butler. You feel the airs and manners, yet you cannot pin them down. So it is with Zen. At times it is taught through allegorical statements, other times through stories and proverbs that illustrate its full meaning which escapes being put into precise words.

Yet Zen can teach you much about getting along with others—an art studied centuries ago by the Indian Buddhas and then adopted by the followers of Zen (and also of Tao, which is also an outgrowth of Buddhism). Since we will hear more about Zen philosophy soon and its use by Orientals in making friends, lets take a look at Zen.

Zen Is a Philosophy

Zen seems to be a philosophy, in part, of not pushing too hard to gain what you want in life.

As Alex King, former *Life* editor, expressed it on Jack Paar's program to those "horizontal listeners and watchers" who nightly watch Paar: "You aim deliberately at a target and miss. You aim again with great care and miss. You become determined, you push hard. Strain. Miss again. Then in disgust you half aim and this time you hit the target smack in the center."

That's popular way of saying, "The Zen way is not to over-do your approach to others, to strain overly-hard to get yourself across with people, but to take it easy and let God and nature take over for you and accomplish your purpose."

As you can see Zen is difficult to explain.

It is hard to put it into words, yet it has been expressed this way: a teacher, when asked "What is Zen?" took his walking stick and spelled the word in the air. The student then saw what Zen was: something written on the wind, seen only for the moment the stick spelled it out.

Zen, says another teacher, is not easily "formalized or expressed." It's nature is to be formless. He says, "In the emptiness of lone meditation your ego rests for a while."

If you will read *Zen for the West* by Sohaku Ogata (Dial Press), or rather study the book for it cannot be read, you will find many descriptions of Zen similar to those in the following paragraphs.

What Zen Can Teach You

Zen is "emancipation from everything, and until you can become formless you can't comprehend Zen." The ultimate goal of Zen is "seeing into self nature," not nature around you, but *inside* you.

That is why meditation is a necessary condition for the perception of Zen, for as you leave your form-body and become formless, you gain a passivity of mind that is so necessary in handling daily problems of life. If you can leave the material world at times (yourself and your surroundings) and just sit silently with yourself, you suddenly resolve all problems just as the target shooter does who suddenly hits the bull's eye when he tries the least.

One teacher explains, "When the cart and horse won't move, you never strike the cart."

"Satori" is the ultimate goal of Zen for that is the moment you see into your self-nature, as Zen teachers would express the art of getting into your subconscious mind. This helps when worries occur and we need to be alone with our thoughts and "to think things out."

There are times to think things out alone, to reach inside and let our self-nature come out. But it cannot be forced.

One allegorical story tells of a cross-legged man sitting by

himself. When asked what he was doing, he said he was strain-
ing to be a Buddha. The teacher then rubbed two bricks together hard. When the cross-legged man asked why he was
doing that, the teacher said, "You cannot rub two bricks together and get a mirror."

Neither can you sit down and say you will find Zen. Or find
friends.

As one teacher has expressed Zen, "Nature is the Mind.
The Mind is Buddha. The Buddha is the Way. The Way is
Zen . . . and Zen is beyond comprehension of the wise and
the ignorant." or it seems that to see directly into your or-
ganized nature is Zen. Put in other words, to understand
yourself is to gain a knowledge that will put yourself across
to others easier.

*

"There is no gate by which to enter Zen," wrote Shuan
Chinken in 1228, and that is expressed in this quixotic way,
"To praise a book by writing a preface is as foolish as
crushing a dry bamboo to get juice." But he advised that you
must grasp each drop of knowledge in life as you go along,
saying, "To let no drop of juice of wisdom fall, for you will
never be able to recover it even if you try to chase it on a
horse that gallops 1,000 miles an hour."

Think that over.

*

Chinken adds, "Nothing that comes in the gate is precious
to the house . . . whatever is casually produced is always
changing."

Think that over.

Chinken goes on to say that a great highway has no gate,
but there are a thousand by-paths.

He also says, "The tongue is boneless—so he talks out of both sides of his mouth."

Many people today retain this faculty of two-tongue talking that the Oriental mind was wary of centuries ago. We should learn to talk straight, out of only one side of our mouth. In this way we gain the respect and confidence of others and get along better with the people around us. We might put it into modern words and say, "Don't be two-faced."

Listen with Your Eyes

Zen, suggests another teacher, is to "listen with your eyes." I like this.

For it gains for you the attention of others.

We cannot listen with our words for when we are talking our ears are closed. We never learn from others when our mouth is open. An art today is to be the good listener first—the good talker second.

We learn not inside the main gate, but along the by-paths.

And the Zen teachers, such as the master Jyoshu, tell you, "When one passes the barrier gate, one walks over heaven and earth." It is at this moment we gain Zen. As one other said, "What is the sound of one pair of clapping hands?"

It is a person, perhaps, complimenting himself.

Other enigmatic thoughts of Zen include such statements as, "The answer is often better than the question." When you think you have finally seen the truth of Zen, "It is the end of the study of Zen."

It means, perhaps, that once you feel you have all the knowledge necessary to get along in life, you are ready to die. You can always learn more and more each day, if your tongue is not boneless and you look beyond the barrier gate and see what might come to you through the by-paths.

Soon Zen Will Be Here

How can the western mind understand Zen, and of what benefit can Zen be in helping us put ourselves across with others—and go places?

That's the question on your mind.

Here are further thoughts. See if they reach you:

Zen, says one master, is "the essence of the Oriental mind." Like a formless stream now running all over Asia, highly practiced today in Japan, it is pentrating into Europe, and will soon reach the American cocktail crowd.

It is a mystical experience in which God and Man are ONE . . . in which subjectivity and objectivity merge. Founded in A.D. 520, it is today a popular study among students, beatniks, and housewives. Many just want to be up on the new, but many will gain true value from a study of this ancient art as well as help in making friends.

One student says Zen is "The self-awakening of what is mindless. It is the mind of mindlessness." The story is then told of a wood chopper who saw a strange animal, called *satori,* with a telepathic power. The wood chopper said to himself, "I must capture the animal" but before he could, the animal, who could read minds, spoke to the man's mind and said, "I see you want to capture me." The man was frustrated.

"I see you are frustrated," said the animal. The man became confused.

"I see you are confused and won't bother with me," the animal went on.

The man then set about hurriedly chopping his wood in bewilderment, and, his mind blank of any thoughts, the axe flew off the handle and killed the animal.

"You see," explains the teacher, "the animal could not read that he was to be killed—for the man's mind had been mindless."

When Zen Takes Hold

Zen takes hold, it is said, of our no-thought.

"Only in eternal calm can Truth reveal itself to you," and this is the substance of Buddha and also of Zen, its outgrowth. Those who protested Buddhism formed Zen and Tao, another off-shoot we will talk about in the next chapter to see how its teaching can help solve today's problems.

Zen has a strange hold on students for the more they know about Zen, the more they seek it, for they realize the great calm it brings to them, helping them in their everyday life of getting along with people.

One master put it this way: "It is easier to get God to move toward me, than me toward God; for it is easier for Him to join me than me Him."

He goes on to say that "disinterest brings God, for everything likes its own habitat."

God's habitat is purity and unity which are due to disinterest.

Therefore, God gives himself to you who are disinterested.

That "disinterest is above Love because Love compels you to suffer for God's sake, and that disinterest makes me sensitive only to God."

This again gets down to the fact that high-pressure to secure success in love, business, or health often defeats its own purpose. You can better attract such hopes and desires through disinterest. Again, the man aiming at the target fails when he strains too hard to hit the bull's eye.

Less violation of the Plimsoll Mark in our lives might be sensible in many cases where we over-do trying to win others to our way of thinking.

It is often better to lead others. Remember the old motto about leading a horse to water.

Put into modern-day rules you might say:

- Invite—don't shove.
- Induce—don't yank.
- Lead—don't push.

Too Much Brilliance Dulls

It seems too much brilliance makes it hard for us to differentiate the trees from the forest, or our aims from our goals. That is why Zen teaches "The man of Zen blunts his intellect and dims his personality, and so shares the dust of common people." Too often we are overly-brilliant for others—and they fail to see our real personality.

RULE: don't try to out-shine others, for then they will fail to see you.

Zen teaches if a thought dwells on anything, it is said to be no-dwelling. "That A is not A—so it is called A." When you understand this you understand Zen.

Reach for *that* thought if you can!

Zen is Elusive

As soon as one tries to get Zen, tell the masters, it escapes one. "It is deathless and it is mindless." Buddhism, its mother philosophy, is a religion of emancipation with Nirvana as its God. Nirvana means to escape transmigration, to become birthless and deathless. Its followers quote such statements as: "all ideas are no ideas; all beings are no beings; you should only cherish thoughts that dwell on form, sound, order, taste, touch."

*

Zen is a matter of experience—not of thought.

*

It avoids taking any one system as its own.

Zen followers believe that enlightenment and ignorance are two sides of the same thing. It is neither long nor short. Large nor small. It slips away. It is space whose bounderies are beyond measurement.

You see Zen is deep. Beyond our ordinary reach.

Yet to penetrate it and try to interpret it into common-day usage in America, is a good healthy mental exercise, one that you can't get by fast reading—only by slow study. As the learned Ogata writes in his book on Zen:

> The great highway has no gate,
> But there are thousands of by-paths
> When one passes the barrier
> One walks over heaven and earth.

It would seem that at least one phase of Zen teaches something each of us can put into daily practice: that is to be well-trained in our habits of work and in living with others. The pusher may feel he gets places faster than the laggard, but in the long run it is easier to convince others to follow our leadership without pushing, shoving or yanking them.

To find the interest of others and then develop that interest yourself, invites likes to likes—disinterest to disinterest—and God comes easier to you because all things like their own habitat best.

Learn what others like, or admire or desire.

This will lead them, instinctively and intuitively, to you.

CHAPTER THOUGHT

Master Jyoshu was once asked by a monk, "Has a dog also a Buddha-nature or not?"
Jyoshu said "Mu." (No.)

ONE WORD SUCCESS FORMULA

ADMIRATION

The one great word of all to win others over—

Give Admiration—and You'll Get Admiration.

24

What Tao is
and how it can help you
win others to your way of
thinking and get you places faster

> *"The grass must bend when the
> wind blows over it."*—Confucius

Tao also came from followers of Buddhism as did Zen.

It has many of the exterior characteristics of Zen. It is not by a rapid-reading that anyone can grasp it in a hurry and become an advocate.

It, too, must be studied to learn modern day adaptations.

Again I go to Ogata, who in turn has gone to others. Here is what I found with some interpretations, about what an ancient philosophy of getting along in the world can do to help us today. A philosophy that has withstood time since A.D. 520 must contain certain basic ingredients worth study.

The Story of Taoism

Here is what you'll read on Tao in ancient books:

Tao that can be defined is not the everlasting Tao.

A student of Tao must, like Zen, blunt the sharpness of his mind, "dim his personality—for in so doing he is not blinded." He can then see better into his inward nature. Again there is the theory that to gain friendships don't be brilliant.

* Be simple.
* Be friendly.

*

The weapon that is forever being sharpened, won't last long.

*

When a house is filled with riches and jade, it is not a secure house. There are innumerable spokes to a wheel, yet the axle hole, small though it be, is necessary to make the many spokes go round and round.

The hollow part of any clay object is as necessary as the clay, and doors and windows are spaced in walls for the same reason.

Forms are useful for their formlessness, and the same with Tao. It is formless.

We Need All Others

Often your very acts today are like the axle of the wheel, the emptiness of the clay pot, yet are important to others. Without the part you play others cannot proceed through life.

We are all dependent upon those around us; while the newsboy is a small cog of the entire newspaper machinery, without him no newspaper could be sold successfully. We must respect the small among us, and not feel that without us it is only they that could not exist. It would be as if the spokes were to say: "We are 36 in number, axle, and you are one small hole. Do our bidding. We are the whole." The axle could well reply, "If I leave you, then where will you go?"

*

Never belittle the humblest around you. They help you function.

*

Tao teaches that if you stand on tiptoe you cannot stand firm.

That if you take long strides you never go far—for self-asserters and self-boosters accumulate no merit.

If your house is filled with riches you only gain the envy of others, teach the men of Tao, who put it in this way, "A surplus of food and rich clothing cause envy in others." Tao therefore does not condone this.

Don't Flaunt Yourself

Neither should you permit the flaunting of wealth.

You may easily be able to afford a better suit, finer shoes, a bigger car, but if you'd win the respect of others, you won't flaunt your riches.

You will not, of course, hide behind a false face of put-on humbleness, for this is as bad as showing off your riches.

You will try to dim yourself in front of others, by having them feel free to expose whatever physical wealth they possess, or demonstrating certain information or talent in which they are well endowed.

Self-boosters are never distinguished.

Nor are people who are overly-polite toward one another, creating suspicions of their motives.

Don't Brag

A Tao sage avoids the superfluous.

He realizes that in any kingdom, your own neighborhood included, people are always changing: first one is ahead, then the other; one is strong at times and weak at others, and it is folly to follow the excesses of any mood, feeling, or thinking.

Generals in war stop fighting after a decisive blow, for they know that to try to win greater supremacy by overdoing a victory only leads to a follow-up depression.

Like the general, be careful not to be overly-proud of your success.

And that gives us two good rules for present day use:

* Never brag of your possessions.
* Be last to brag about yourself.

These rules will help people to like you.

Avoid the Mirror

A person of greatest virtue is not conscious of it and therefore remains virtuous; the same is true of any person skilled in a trade. Once he becomes conscious of how good he is, he is on the way to personal defeat unless he can remain master of his success.

The actor who struts in front of a mirror soon sees his personality change from one well-liked to one well-hated.

Take your victories and successes with bland pleasure only.

Be humble in your greatest moments. Let others do the back patting, for if you pat your own back you are apt to break an arm. If you pin a rose on your own lapel, you are apt to prick the finger with the hidden thorn that is inside all victories.

*

So you see that the teaching of Tao remain modern, even though they were written and spoken centuries ago. These same Taoisms are in Zen and in Buddhism, expressed in slightly different ways. All three seem to aim at the same goal much as other religions follow the same approximate roads to eternity.

The Art of Contentment

Let's go further into the sage remarks of Tao and Zen:
The content man is always satisfied.
The greatest of all sins is to have overt desires that are continuously tempting, for a follower of Zen avoids satiation. The one who says he will try dope just once, finds himself trying it just twice, then thrice, and soon he is "hooked."
Giving in to harmful desires is bad.
Merchandise your desires as you'd merchandise your business, or your pleasure.

*

Nothing hurts more than disappointment.

*

Therefore watch your goals in life. Don't extend them too far ahead of you. A little at a time is good, so you can keep moving forward, and not be going backwards with disappointment. The man who tries to eat everything at one meal soon has a stomach ache. The person who eats a little at a time of life finds life won't give him a belly ache.

Winning by Inaction

Tao teaches that learning consists in adding to your stock of knowledge, and diminishing the stock daily, for by a gradual cancelling out of knowledge you reach a state wherein nothing is left undone.

Therefore, as Ogato puts it, "An empire can be won by inaction. Whoever needs to act in order to win is not worthy of it."

I admit you must reach for that thought.

But it means again that the principle of over-pressuring, overly-pushing, pulls you backwards in life, and doesn't extend you forward.

*

Tao is taking life in calmness.

The person who knows how to be content in life with what he has, or plans soon to get, enjoys a long life. The person who knows where to stop is free of danger, teach the Tao sages. One who knows how to be content is free from disgrace.

One writing teaches: Those who know Tao do not speak about it; those who speak about it do not know it.

Translated into modern day philosophy, I'd say that again the person who pats his own back and overly pushes himself forward moves backward and not forward in life's march.

People who know are the ones who know better than to convince others how much they know. They are content to sit in the knowledge of their being good, and so have no inferiority complexes ever prodding them on for recognition and false praise.

Froth on Chocolate Sodas

When you see one stroking his mustache in glee as he brags of winning a battle, a love, or a challenge, that one is to be watched. He is putting froth on a chocolate soda for he knows the soda is weak in chocolate and will need stage dressing to get the mind of the buyer off the lack of chocolate.

A good steak needs no sizzle except to attract attention to its goodness; and a bad steak can sizzle all day long, and have no repeat business.

Therefore be first to get in line, but also first to permit others to proceed before you if that is their desire. One who side-steps the other, temporarily, often sees the plunger get tripped up along the line.

Don't Be Tripped Up

When a government is tolerant, teaches a sage of Tao, then people are honest; but when it interferes, people become cunning.

Many a foot is ready to trip you up in life if you are intolerant. If you are too demanding, arrogant, difficult to impress, others will find subtle ways of tripping you up.

On the other hand, if you are tolerant of others, realizing we are all strong and all weak at the same time, but maybe on different things, then you encourage others to give you a helping hand and not a tripping foot.

Beware of mild applause.

It is better you get no applause from others, than a mild applause, for that is a disgrace. It means the other person not only disagrees or dislikes you, but does so with a vengeance.

The Art of Moderation

Moderation is always the best. You rule men and your own life easier through moderation, for "it is the shortest cut by which a man can return to his original state . . . through what is called the repeated accumulation of virtue."

Say the sages: "A child's bones are weak and soft, but its

grasp is firm. He can cry all day without becoming hoarse, because of the harmony of his constitution."

You can go places faster through harmony than discord, a present-day follower of Tao might say, explaining that violence always comes from discord. A person must steel himself against gain or loss, and not let it throw him into disharmony. If he can do this he can be a good follower of Tao or Zen—or just his own present-day ideas—for the one who doesn't fall apart when trouble comes, but faces it firmly, wins.

In modern-day idiomatic language: learn to roll with the blows.

Retreat to Go Forward

The men of Tao say: "I would rather be the host than the guest when war is declared. I would rather retire a foot than advance an inch."

That is good business tactic, too: Be quick to bow. Quicker to nod in agreement. For often in retreating a step through admission, or allowing the other to proceed, you gain strength to go forward faster at a later time.

An engine backs up its freight cars to tighten them before it can move forward.

It is often better to back yourself and tighten. Then when you begin to move forward, like the train, the cars won't be bumping and rumbling and holding you back.

It is often well to retreat in the face of an angry or upset man. Better than to assert yourself, and buck him, bow out and return another day; nod yourself into success.

Learn the art of shaking the head up and down—not sidewise.

The person who knows his limitations, goes places.

As Tao puts it, "Not to know, but to think one knows, is a disease. If you know when you are ill, you are free of disease."

Tabulate Your Handicaps

Too many people today fail to know their handicaps and limitations, yet if they were to know and admit them, they'd gain strength. The person who realizes he must stay in the wheel chair for life becomes stronger and keener through the experience. The blind become better hearers; and those with admitted loss of hearing become keener observers.

You will never lose friends by admitting a weakness.

It is better to say, "I am sorry I do not know, but I can find out," than to attempt to answer on subjects beyond you.

People like failures. They detest successes.

To win people, admit a weakness. To lose them, brag.

The brave die while the cowards live. When people are not afraid of death, how can capital punishment frighten them?

Read something into those ancient thoughts.

*

Nothing is softer than water. Yet when it multiplies, it gives energy that is boundless.

Nothing replaces it.

*

The sage does not store up knowledge for himself, but the more he gives to others the more he gets for himself.

"Sincere words are not fine and fine words are not sincere. Good men are not eloquent and eloquent men are not good."

Thus teach the sages of Tao.

Go Farther on the Road

The strategies and techniques of getting along with people, is one that the Asian mind has long perceived, and one too long kept away from the modern world. There have always been difficult times in history, and wars, but there is more conflict today than ever before because of man's proceeding further away from the basic principles of getting along with people. Therefore let's go once more into history and see what other teachings of Tao (and Zen and Buddhism) can give to use for our daily requirements in getting along with one another.

Many ancient teachers explain many times that "you must go beyond the barrier gate to see things in proper light."

This expressed in modern language might be, "Often the real thing is not where it seems to be. To proceed farther down the road will bring you to reality."

Only too often do we listen to someone complain. But we must not always dwell on his complaint. It is perhaps better to listen well until the complainer goes into stage two, and tells you the real things on his mind; that is why a good complaint department manager will also say, "Is that your only complaint?" This invites the complainer to give further reasons for his unhappiness, and often the hidden reason of the complaint comes out.

Everyone has two reasons for not doing something for you: the reason he gives, and the real reason.

It is important to know that you must go beyond the obvious barrier gate and penetrate to the depths.

As a master teacher of Tao will tell you, "By opening the third eye, you will understand."

It often takes three eyes to penetrate the thinking of the other.

We Don't All Wear Beards

When asked why a Buddhist had no beard, the sage Wakun said words to this effect as translated by Ogata:

Don't discuss a dream
In the presence of a fool
The barbarian has no beard,
What nonsense this is.

Men are often not what they seem. That is why the more experience one has in meeting people, the sooner he sees their real self behind their cloak or beard, and thus in understanding can sell them better or get over his wishes faster.

All prophets don't wear beards.

All salesmen don't have brief cases.

All doctors don't wear stethoscopes.

Questions Are Answers

When certain Buddhist teachers want to make a point to a beginner, they often say to a foolish question, "Your question is your answer."

How often we waste time asking questions to which we have the answer, or know there is no answer, or the answer is in the question itself. This marks us as stupid to others. It is better to follow the old philosophy and not make minor remarks just to make conversation.

*

Silence often sells us to others faster than conversation.

*

Don't Be a "Rice-Bag"

In the language of Zen a "rice-bag" is a fellow who is a good-for-nothing.

He may be liked—he may not be. But it is well that you discern the rice-bags from the real fellows around you.

If you have this faculty, you will get along in the 20th Century as did the followers of Zen in the 4th Century.

*

If you cannot see the truth, you cannot convince another.

*

"Whoever gossips will be gossiped about."
Need more be added to this Zen philosophy?

Tao Is Ordinary Thinking

When asked how he could know when he attained Tao, a hermit was told, "Ordinary mind is Tao."
"How then do I get it?"
"As soon as you try to get it you'll miss it."
"Then how do I know when I get Zen without trying to get it?"
The answer then was very simple, for the teacher said, "When one attains Tao that one will see it as clearly as one sees the universe."
The hermit thought a moment then replied, "Then what is the use of arguing about it?"
And that is good philosophy to give to perennial arguers, always debating one another. Always making claims—Always putting forth pet ideas, forcing them on others.
For why argue a point that becomes clear when each sees the light? It is better to listen one another out, to see if the facts themselves won't clear the situation without need of arguing.

Let facts speak for themselves.
Let basic truths clear the air.
Let truth tell the truth.
No one ever wins a heated argument.

Talking With Tongues

When a great One was asked why he never stood up, without using his feet, the answer was simple, "The tongue has nothing to do with speaking."

Yet how often we talk to others with our tongue alone.

We make fast sentences formed only by our boneless tongues, without once seeking the aid of our mind.

What wonder then that a person who habitually "runs at the mouth" has little respect for others.

Watch closely for the words of wisdom of one who speaks little, but when he does, talks with his mind and not his tongue.

To distinguish the mind-speaker from the tongue-talker in life helps you get along better; for you will not become upset with the tongue speaker, nor follow his advice down wrong roads.

The greatest of all traits in getting places in life is to be able to weigh words of others, to be able to weed out the truths from the half-truths, the rumors from the facts, the gossip from the honest words.

Don't Chatter Glibly On

When one fails to win the other, it is often best to retreat temporarily rather than press the point. Little can be gained in the heat of an argument. Little can be found in heated words. As a Zen sage puts it:

Truly there is little point
In chattering glibly on.

So you see, reaching back into the 4th Century to find ways of getting along in the 20th Century is not a foolish move.

At first one wonders what application Zen and Tao and

Buddhism has in today's commerce; yet through creative use of the imagination, one can adopt these philosophies of the orientals and learn better how to guide our actions to win others to our side.

*

There are time when silence doesn't hold.

Times when you must assert yourself, for as a sage once said, "Silence is either concerned with affirmation or negation."

*

Over-talk is bad.

The one who continues to explain his errors is at fault, for then he exaggerates them. It is best then to remain silent.

Repetition spoils the merit of a superior man.

When to Give In

There are times, too, to give in.

Dogmatically fighting for your thoughts, in the face of obstinate objection, is trying to blow the wind away from you. It cannot be accomplished.

In forcing yourself or your thoughts on others, you may do more damage than to bow the head, temporarily, in defeat to gain strength.

Although he saved his nose,
He lost his eye. What a pity!

Which Banner Is Moving?

Ogato, the great teacher of Zen and Tao interpretations, brings out a good story in saying that one man said the banner was moving and the other said it was the wind moving.

Too often it is hard to discern which is moving about you;

so relax and study the situation a moment. Then when you see which is moving, you will know how to move.

In modern words: *don't go off half-cocked.*

In placing blame, in trying to sell a group, be sure which one controls the wind.

You can often waste time trying to get your point across with the wrong person, who often is the one who talks most but dominates least. The silent partner in a business or in a home often controls the real purse strings.

Learn to see beyond the barrier gate.

*

As the questions were alike,
So were the answers.

*

Perhaps the best explanation of Buddhism, and its outgrowths of Zen and Tao, is the remark given to a monk who asked, "What is Buddha?" and was told, "There is no mind, no Buddha." And to which another then commented, "To see the truth here is the end of Zen study."

How to Catch Greedy Fish

Another says, "Wisdom is not Tao." And transmigration was described once as moving from hotel to hotel.

There is another saying among Taoists and that is: "When you fish in a swift stream, you catch greedy fish."

How true this is in our lives today. We reach out for fast-action money, we grab too far up the social ladder, and in taking so much at a leap we are greedy.

What happens to the greedy? The same as to the fish in the swift stream, "As soon as they open their mouths to grab the bait, their lives are taken away."

Greed is a disease.

It can destroy as surely as gossip.

If you play among skunks, soon you acquire the odor of one, as you do if you sell perfume. You will find that proper association gives you better airs, and frees you of greed.

Never want beyond your reach.

The gaining of it may bring on greed.

It is better to play in quiet waters.

*

You must reach to understand these philosophies of Tao, for they are not written. It is not a religion, it is almost not a philosophy—but a Way. An experience as is all of our lives.

For example, when one asked a monk what to do about his mind that was so troubled, the monk said, "Bring me your mind and I will set it at rest."

The man thought a moment then replied, "I cannot find my mind."

The monk replied, "Then I have set it at peace."

Often when you search for your worries, your troubles, to bring them into light for help of others, you cannot find them. The search to locate what mentally ailed you is a cure in itself.

Sit down and examine your worries. Dig for your troubles. The very work of defining them often dispels them.

This is a great Way—a modern Way—that Tao taught centuries ago.

Learn to Speak Quickly

There is another saying of the Orientals and that is, "Don't describe it in words, don't describe it without words. Speak quickly."

Many interpretations can be attached to this, but I like to

think that a person who overly-thinks when asked a question is often weighing which side of his boneless tongue to use.

If you'd impress others, speak quickly.

When given a choice, make up the mind fast—for in hesitation you worry the other person who wonders why you have hesitated—for you had a choice of words and no-words. To have hesitated showed you were trying to decide what to say to benefit you, not to give information.

You will win many people by speedy answers. At least they'll know you as honest, even though your speedy reply may require modification later on.

Nothing can be hidden or secreted behind speedy words.

*

"Losing games is also fun," is part of Tao teachings.

There is certainly one way to gain immediate admiration of others: lose gracefully. Lose with fun.

People detest perpetual winners. No one feels comfortable around a Tin God.

Learn the trick of losing gracefully.

To Lift the Soul

Sekiso, the master, once asked, "How can you climb a step above the top of a pole 100 feet high?" He had wondered since it was often said in his day that a man who jumps through a hoop on top of a pole is truly the great one. So Sekiso wanted to know how it could be done.

It can be done by being a little better than others in soul, body, health, mind. Having more respect, more concern for others, puts you over the top of the pole. Helping others beyond requirement—going out of your way to offer aid, puts you a step above the 100 foot pole.

See where you can take that one extra step in life.

It will give your soul a lift.

Aims of Tao

It is said over and again that the only aim of Zen (or Tao or Buddhism) is to see your own nature, for when you understand your own nature, you are free of life and death.

Spoken centuries ago, these words could well be spoken today in any house, in any office, in any cocktail lounge or tea party. The words are as ageless as is Zen and Tao and Buddhism.

We learn from the past.

Never mind your path. Just avoid the blatant main barrier gate. Go beyond it a little to the by-paths that help make you outstanding in life, for people in the by-paths go places faster.

And lastly, let Ogato, the teacher, leave you with one more thought the 20th Century to get along with others, and sell yourself better:

> The goal is reached before the first step is taken
> The talk is over before a word has been said.
> Even if you know how to take the first step
> Remember that there is another way up the mountain.

The greatest of all friend-making
sentences you can ever use to promote
goodwill and go places in life:

"YOU DID A GREAT JOB!"

25

Yoga—and how
this oriental philosophy
can be used by anyone
to help him get along
better in life

> *"Success is a ladder which cannot be climbed*
> *with your hands in your pockets."*

Yoga, at first blush, had no place in a book on human relations.

Then you delve into this Oriental philosophy and find it is far more than an exercise of the body; it is a philosophy of the soul to help you get along better with mankind.

Yoga teaches more the relaxation of the physical being it is also of the mind and the soul, and has a place in the life of anyone who wants to go places on his own Main Street.

Yoga teaches, among many things, that you must not look for a return of your love, kindness or gifts to others; for if you expect a return, you are not truly a follower of Yoga. And that's a good philosophy for our daily business.

Other teachings of Yoga, applicable to present day living, include:

241

- Jealousy drapes love in chains.
- Outworn ideas are like ghosts.
- Strive for simplicity.
- Forego pleasures only of the moment.

All are mottos that would fit on any business man's desk.

For you can readily see that this ancient philosophy can be today's common sense way of getting along with others.

Certainly, if we are jealous of others, we get nowhere in life. Being jealous is no way to gain a promotion, make a sale, with somebody over to our way of thinking; for jealousy is like a worn out idea, a ghost, that neither strives for simplicity, nor forgoes the pleasures only of the moment.

This story of Yoga can help you over life's bumps.

What Exactly is Yoga?

Yoga is thought to be merely an exercise, sitting cross-legged. That's the Western idea of it, but it goes much further.

It goes into the practice of the physical to strengthen the mind and soul; for Yoga gives body energy to produce mental energy.

Here are some teachings of Yoga to explain what it is:

> The body is a good servant but a bad master.
> This means we know little about how to make the body work to give us the mental energy we need.
> Yoga says:
> A saying is saved by its truth.
> And there is another good bit of common sense in these teachings:
> It is better to write a story than to read one.
> Bad luck is happiness we don't understand.

You can readily apply a modern adaptation of these sayings; for too often we sit back and let others write the stories of life, and we endeavor to live them. Much better to have attempted, crude as it may be, to write a few chapters in our own book of life, for personal experience—then we learn from practical experience and not theoretical book learning.

And to believe that bad luck is hard luck is ridiculous. Only too often as we look back on our lives we see the upward turning point came from what we at the time called bad luck. It was good luck in disguise.

Yoga Is Really Modern Philosophy

Yoga is said to organize life to beat death.

One teaching is that Yoga (and it applies to Zen, Tao and Buddhism), is that it cannot be learned from books; but, rather, it is more our instincts guiding us to God, our ultimate goal in living.

Yoga teaches one to "not think."

By this is meant you should sit and not think as you concentrate. Once you can thus control your mind, you can practice Yoga in any of its 84 or so forms of sitting crosslegged, in the many postures that relax the body and therefore relax the mind and permit thought to flow freely, letting us make full use of our subconscious mind.

That is why people think Yoga is exercise. It is not, unless you think of complete relaxation to permit the flow of thoughts, as an exercise, and perhaps it is rightly so.

As with the other Oriental philosophies, Yoga cannot be pursued. It goes down what is called the "path of non-pursuit," meaning you cannot chase it—you must invite it to come to you through passivity and not through shove and push that often gets us nowhere in life.

It teaches one to desire nothing, deny nothing.

You must cast out pride, possession, vanity and shame to

be a real follower of Yoga, to release your soul so you can get along better in life with those around you.

How Can This Help You?

Yoga, brought up to a practical, modern use, can help you in these ways:

1. *Yoga can give you physical energy to meet life's aches and pains.* One way to lose energy is to spin your wheels on needless chores that others can do easier and cheaper, such as fixing TV sets, laying rugs, painting houses—assignments that often end us up in a turmoil of nerves. It is often less expensive for the experts to take over and give us time to do what we excel in.

2. *Yoga says that silence teaches as much as sound words.* Often we like to get away by ourselves and just think, and that is good for us. It clears out our cobwebs. It relaxes our nerves. We can then "talk" to ourselves in silence, and when we return from such meditation we have often found the solutions to our difficulties. So learn the great Oriental art of meditation—talking things out by ourselves.

3. *Yoga teaches you to control the body to control the mind.* The Trappist monks sit silently, and so do the Quakers. It is not necessary to always be talking to someone to be learning. If you were to join the School of Pythagoras at Crotana, you'd be required not to speak for 2 years but to listen.

As someone once said, "Speech is silver—silence golden."

Therefore try getting away from it all occasionally. Often more can pass between people in silence than in heated conversation, however eloquent the conversation may be.

There are times to say, "Let's retire and think it over." In so doing, people then return with new concepts, new ideas, new thinking.

Love Is Called Polarity

If a boy holds a dog's tail and the dog tries to get away, who then is pulling the tail—the boy or the dog?

That's a question in Yoga.

It is a question to ask yourself. If you are pulling one way against a friendship, and another is pulling the other way—just who is pulling the friendship?

An interesting way to look at life, isn't it?

Polarity is often given as another word for love. It is the chemistry of two things going toward each other for union, that's what love is. Yoga therefore means "union of little and all things." All color is a modification of white—all sounds are modifications of one tone that the Chinese frequently called "the great tone."

So all life is made up of the one you.

Many people fear silence. That is why they babble to each other in the dark. A fear that at times makes them sing, hum or whistle in the dark. People often use meaningless words with one another when fear strikes them, fear of losing a deal, a friend, or a loved one.

Yet here is where silence would find the cure.

Laugh At Yourself

Yoga teaches that if you can laugh at yourself, you've attained your true height.

You are able, when you laugh at yourself, to say to trouble, "So what?" It is often called the "So what?" philosophy.

There are time when to sit and laugh at yourself brings you complete relaxation and the resultant peace and contentment self-laughter brings on.

That's a mighty good business principle for present day useage.

"The sage does nothing and everything is accomplished."
Schopenhauer put it this way: "Regard the present as already
set."

If we moderns thought this same way, life would have less
anger and discontent.

Our point of view may often differ with others, but as a
whole does not greatly differ.

Shoes, for example, were said to have been discovered
when a king cut his foot on a stone in a road. He at once ordered the Grand Vizier to pave the roads of the kingdom
with carpets. But being an impossibility, the Grand Vizier
conceived the idea of shoes and sold the idea to the king with
the proverb:

"To him who wears a shoe it is as though the world were
covered with leather."

What is your point of view?

Maybe you and the others are, after all, thinking alike only
you have different ways of doing the job.

If the impossible to teach of you is impossible, then make
the impossible possible.

Don't try too hard. Instead, conceive a mutual idea as of
"shoes." You may lighten your work with the idea, avoiding
the loss of a friend through a disagreement that is no disagreement at all when looked upon from a new light, a new
angle . . . a new twist.

Learn to Think "Unattached"

Yoga teaches detachment.

To understand your problem, you must un-attach yourself
from both sides.

In fact, being un-attached to either side often makes the
game of life more fun, just as at a ball game, you can often
have more enjoyment sitting disinterested on the sidelines.

So try sitting that way on some problem that is confronting you and your opponent. See if sitting on the sideline doesn't clear up the situation.

Avoid Any Excesses

The Yoga follower has some 84 ways of relaxing his mind and soul, so never does one of the 84 ways in excess.

"The only golden rule is that there is no golden rule," say devotees of Yoga.

This is a pretty way to say with words, "Nothing in excess." Or, "Be moderate in all you do."

Excess of fun—leisure, love, work—of anything—leads to satiation. And satiation is getting too much of anything, and this sours your appetite.

The child seldom chews the sucker. He sucks it. He licks it lightly—thus prolonging the flavor and the desire to lick on.

A dog often eats a little at a time of his bowl of food, walking around the bowl on and off, to prolong the delight.

Try this in your life. Take a little at a time. It lasts longer.

The 84 Yoga Positions

There are said to be some 84 positions of Yoga to relax the body and the brain. However, the two main positions are all most devotees actually practice. They are called the Lotus and the Half-Lotus postures.

The main purpose of the postures is to strengthen the spine, to put the body into a position of utmost relaxation, so that the vibrations of the inner body can be most free. The soul is then at ease, and the body also breathes easier.

One rule, though, is that these practices must be done *privately,* so as not to be interrupted by others.

Nor must they be practiced after any excess of work or eating. I will not attempt, for it does not fit this study, to give you the forms of Yoga, except for one as given by Dr. S. J. Singh, who writes:

> "Sit with the body perfectly straight after placing the right foot in the cavity between the left thigh and the calf, and the left foot in the cavity between the right thigh and the calf . . . remaining unmoved like a post, directing the eyes to the spot in the middle of the brows."

This is one of the main positions of Yoga that will give you utmost relaxation, to sit and meditate.

This is the position often seen in statues or pictures of Buddha, with his chin held high. His eyes gaze steadily into space to invite thought that is undisturbed by worldly surroundings.

It is certainly a posture that will invite your energy to create, so that once you stand up you will feel as a new person. And you are.

*

If from Yoga you have learned just this one rule of gaining energy to fight on in life, you have learned considerable of this ancient and most honorable way of rejuvenating a run-down body and brain.

*

"Beware of food murdered by a chef," is an Oriental proverb for eating simply.

It means you can butcher ideas the same way, destroying thought and clarity.

*

The Sphinx is a picture of relaxation.

So are your dog and cat when they lie, on a cold day, in the sunlight streaming through your window.

The Sphinx relaxes all who look at it; so do the cat and dog. Therefore, learn to relax in front of others, and watch them follow suit.

Why the Straight Spine?

Why the straight spine of the Yoga advocate? Of the Sphinx?

It is said that the spine is the "lightning rod of the body and the brain."

For it brings down heavenly thoughts to relax the body, saving our strength for things that require strength.

Thus the famous postures of Yoga permit us to breathe and to gain proper strength to carry on with our life; for the air is taken into our lungs in proper manner, unhindered, especially if the chin is held high and the chest is out.

The true posture of a successful person!

No singer really gives the fullest until this posture is achieved; nor any speaker; nor any person trying to sway another to his way of thinking.

Proper posture is a requisite to proper thinking—and the person who slumps over a chair at a meeting seldom sells others.

So learn these tricks of Yoga.

One good book is by Claude Bragon, *Yoga For You* (Knopf). In the book Bragon says in part:

"Sit upright. The body must be a straight line else it breathes feebly. The spinal cord needs to be undisturbed, to be straight so as not to pinch nervous energy. Thus the nerves are controlled—and the breath comes naturally."

The next step is the control of the nerves which control our respiratory organs, like a master switch. This means having proper thoughts that do not cramp nervous energy. This makes us unexcited, relaxed, open to ideas—not tangled up in fears, tensions, frustrations.

Only a nervous system so free can properly control breath, and the ultimate thinking of others around us.

This is the posture of a harmonized body and soul.

A Great Yoga Trick

One way as taught by Yoga to completely relax the body is to first hold the left nostril tight with your thumb. Breathe deeply.

Then do the same with the right nostril.

This makes sure your breathing is normal and not constricted. It is often practiced with the Yoga devotee holding his breath in his lungs to completely fill the lungs to every corner; and when he exhales, out comes all inner poisons of breath from every corner of the lungs.

The action completely relaxes the body and its nervous system.

It puts a fighter, a singer, a lecturer, a lawyer—or one trying to win over another—into the best condition for what lies ahead of him. He is then mentally alert and able to grasp everything and anything coming his way.

This Yoga exercise, in its many variations, trains the body to breathe properly at all times under all conditions.

As expressed in oriental wordage, "Thus use doth breed a habit in a man."

The habit of proper breathing to give us vim, vigor and GO! To get places in life.

Yoga Teaches Rhythm in Life

One result of Yoga is to gain rhythm in life.

It is often called "self-mastery." The control of yourself.

Anything that is not moving harmoniously will set up a

vibration that soon, as in your car engine, will rattle bolts loose. So with the body.

Harmony is love without discord that burns energy.

What is love? you ask again. And this time I give Swedenborg's statement: "Man knows there is love, but he does not know what love is."

One ancient wit puts love this way: "Kiss, couple, beget."

There is no sexual problem in the animal kingdom where the rhythm of nature is unbroken. Animals never indulge in over-sex that uses up the calcium in our bodies in what Orientals call "sweetest experience of all human relations."

It all gets back to, "Nothing in excess." "Moderation."

Yoga, by the way, is a Sanskrit word: the word *yug* from which comes the English word "conjugal," pertaining to marriage.

*

Summed up, Yoga is the Oriental philosophy that teaches, "You find yourself by losing yourself."

It is harmony of body and soul: A big secret that we, today, may well practice to get along better with others.

Yoga teaches meditation—and meditation cleanses the mind.

Find your place in life for moments of quiet meditation that will rejuvenate your body and brain, and you will go further in finding and reaching your goal.

Over the door of the temple of Apollo at Delphi is a motto: "Man, know thyself, to be divine."

There is another Hermetic teaching: "There exists a harmonious and unbroken sequence to all things."

I guess that sums up Yoga, and how it can in these modern times of excess stress and tension and strain help you get along freer and better in your chosen tasks.

Be harmonious in life—gain energy, and go places.

"A man without a smiling face must not open a shop."

WHAT'S A SALESMAN?

"Anyone who can sell anything to Jack Benny and make a profit is a salesman"—Fred Allen

*

"Traveling salesmen" were known in 2500 B.C., for even then the art of selling yourself to others was found important to go places in life.

*

Centuries ago merchant guilds forced their members to carry protective armor, a bow and a dozen arrows—but today we need only a pleasant manner, well chosen words, and a sense of good humor to get along with people.

*

At one time a seller carried a pack on his back and a knife up his sleeve. Today sellers of ideas or things merely show friendliness, honesty and an ability to get along with all sorts of people.

*

"Attention getters" were used years ago to command interest of people. One man carried a jumping Mexican bean. Many got attention with an Indian. How do you get the favorable attention of people whom you want to win over to your way of thinking?

*

We are all anxious to gain attention of others. Paul Revere used a bell!

*

Don't sell the steak—sell the sizzle!

*

People like familiar things, old as they may be. The new annoys them. Ben Bodne, owner of the "ancient" Algonquin Hotel in New York City, has remodeled it many times, but the interior decorators and carpenters are instructed to "make the new look familiar and friendly." One customer complained. He said, "The water closets look the same, Mr. Bodne, but they are now silent!"

*

The affable "drummer" with the big cigar, the hanging watch chain, and the latest jokes, is now replaced by men (and women) who win others to their way of thinking by well chosen words.

*

26

Here are instant ways
to lose friendships
and alienate people!

> *"You'll have bad luck if you leave the
> broom that way—bend the bristles, too."*

Way 1:
  Be a crab.

Become a professional pessimist among your friends.
Be quick to say, "The world is coming to an end." Be fast to
find fault with our President, or anyone else in the government. Always gripe about the way the boss treats you, your
club, or some organization. Be a fault finder—and you'll soon
be finding a need to find new friends.

*

Way 2:
  Be a milktoast in life.

Hesitate to spend a dime for anything. Be tight.
Tell friends, "Well, I don't believe I can afford to go out."
You can, but you are miserly about your money.
When the collection box is passed, look the other way; if

caught, drop in a handful of noisy coins (pennies) .

Be quick to refuse a collection for some member of the office who is getting married, or is in a hospital. Refuse all such good-will requests.

Assume the "poor boy" attitude—and you'll be poor in friends.

*

Way 3:

Be always "on the line."

Never cross a street against a red light; never over-spend; never go without your eight hours sleep each night.

Be a righteous *bore.*

This is no plea to disregard the law or to be a beatnik in so-ciety, but there are times when to play hookey or kick up your heels brands you as a regular guy.

Be a strictly "on the line" guy—and you'll be strictly out of good fellowship instantly.

*

Way 4:

Never go into debt!

Live within the utter limits of your income. Never once fling the *dinero* around. Never once waste it by buying someone a drink, or taking them out to lunch.

For if you go in debt, well you'll have to work hard to make it up. Many a millionaire, when asked what gave him ambition, said: "I went in debt and had to work like hell to get out of it!"

He did—and kept up the pace and ended with a fortune. But don't you. Be an old skinflint—and you'll skin yourself out of palmanship.

*

Way 5:

Don't Seek Power!

Look what happened to Hitler. Peron. Castro. Look what hap-pens to anyone who lets POWER rule his life.

You'll never get places, but brother, no one will declare you to be power-mad . . . in fact, no one will want to be around you. They'll perhaps let you hold the line down, and end up Mr. Average.

*

Way 6:
Invite yourself to friends' homes.

Drop into business offices, into homes, saying, "I was just in the neighborhood so I thought I'd drop in."
You'll get faint smiles. Weak cheer. You'll get around—well, until friends spot you coming down the street and turn out the lights and lock the front door.
"The uninvited guest is worse than a Tartar," say the Orientals.

*

Way 7:
Find fault with the mate!

Freud said: "The basic motivation behind everything a man does is the desire to please a woman."
So if you are a woman, don't be pleased with the mate. Find fault. Make him discouraged.
You won't have to bother with him for too long around the house; he'll end up in Tahiti having his back scratched!

*

Way 8:
Make others feel unimportant.

Don't let your man be head of the house. You take over the job. Make him *unimportant.*
Make people who work with you feel unimportant, even though psychologists say that importance is the greatest single motivation a person has to become a success.
Run things your way at all times, and at all times you'll be in need of help!

*

I might add something about nagging wives; about disgruntled husbands—but these are classic ways to lose happiness too often written about to mention.

I could fill a book with unhappy people, but instead, look
around and see the happy ones: Churchill, whose wife didn't
nag him; Ford, whose wife was understanding when, in mid-
years, he decided to put all his money and time into making
a car, gambling all his security.

These men had "companions" as well as mates. They had
understanding companions since "behind everything a man
does is the desire to please a woman." Happy men, inspired
by the women in their lives, have gone places.

Let the boss be head of the office; let the husband be head
of the house; let the wife be head of the kitchen—let others
head up things, for that is good leadership.

Listen Well to Others

Be understanding of others.

Listen well to what they have to say. Be quick to nod in
appreciation of the other person.

*

"For women to bear children isn't easy, but to keep quiet
is really hard."

*

"The slower you drive in life, the further you get," as any
person who "gets along" with others well knows. And "if we
eat the bad seed now, we won't have to worry about what
kind of crop we have next year." Our words do seed themselves, grow beauty or grow weeds. And remember, "At the

bottom of the wine bottle you'll always find dregs."

Just don't drink so far.

Be Quick to Give

Be quick to give assignments to others, remembering that it will make them feel important. The load is lighter that rests on two pair of shoulders, instead of only your own.

Be quick to give—for "the hand that always takes never tires of its work;" and those who constantly give do not have this worry in life. The hand that gives never tires. But know *where* and *when* and *what* to give, for there is still another ancient adage: "Giving a present to the rich is like giving water to the sea."

Lastly remember to avoid being avaricious. Practice the proverb: "Counting other people's money will never make YOU rich!"

"Live a hundred years, learn a hundred years—and you still die a fool!"

A Short, Short Story

The Pills The Doctors Cannot Give

I asked Andy Patton one day how he appeared so chipper. What new tonic, what new pill was he taking?

He told me: "I'm taking a pill the doctors cannot give me."

My eyes opened wide, so did my ears, to learn what this magic new pill was that had stepped-up the health, the vim and vigor of this former district attorney.

Andy smiled, for he knew what he had to say would surprise me. He said, "My pill is the out-of-doors, the sunshine, the air."

"What's so mystical about that pill," I almost grunted, having expected to learn something new about a magic potion from the Orient.

"Doctors cannot give you this pill," said Andy. "They can only prescribe it, but you must find it yourself and you won't on the shelves of a pharmaceutical house."

I began to catch on.

I saw what Andy meant. It was homely, simple, almost corny medical advice he had given me—but as with other magic elixirs, it is always that way.

The best pills are the simplest.

The best pills are inexpensive.

I have known men who lop up the latest information on pills, who have boxes of them in their medicine cabinets, and pretty silver pill cases to tote around in their pockets. Walking pharmaceutical stores. They are always stuffing a new pill in a new color down their throats, to give them pep to get places in life.

Yet nature has more and better pills.

What is more, these pills nature dishes out are free. They are yours for the asking.

How do you get them?

Andy Patton has this answer too: "I have a camp at Lake Grapevine. My wife and I go there week ends, and get out on the lake, into the sun—getting vitamins and minerals direct from the source: nature."

The man talked medical sense, as he told me: "At night we take a little hike around the neighborhood. On week ends when I don't go to the camp, I get out into my back yard for an hour or so among the weeds and the flowers, bending my back, bending my knees, getting needed exercise."

I nodded Andy on.

"I own a rocking chair, too. My friends smile as I rock in it, but you know—it's good exercise. It keeps your knees oiled up, it keeps your back in motion, something easy chairs don't do."

Andy was still right.

"You know," he went on, "the easy den chair is the curse of the middle-aged. I get glued to a TV program in a comfortable chair, and when I try to get up my bones yell out at me. But when I get up from the rocker, well only the rocker yells. I, too, am an advocate of the Rocking Chair Way to health and happiness—another pill the docs can't give you."

It all sounded sensible to me.

And it looked sensible for Andy—for the pallor of a recent operation had left him. He again looked like the navy commander he was during World War II. He stood taller. He smiled broader. He began to go places again in life, and his legal office in Dallas, Texas, is now being filled with potential clients attracted to a man who knows the health rules to attract friends and business.

How?

By the pill the doctors cannot give!

27

The magic ingredient
that lies in all of us
that does most to make us rich

"Everybody lives by selling something."

I was impressed with Alex Osburn's little booklet he issued some time ago called, "The Gold Mine Between the Ears." Osburn, now retired, once headed one of the world's largest advertising agencies and knows whereof he speaks.

It is Osburn's philosophy that everybody is born with a magic ingredient to make money and go places in life: *your ability to think.*

He then goes on to show how creative imagination is not possessed by a favored few—but by all of us, and it made me feel good to know I, too, possessed this magical ingredient to get up the ladder of success.

On reading Alex Osburn's golden booklet, you are really impressed with one thing: everybody is born with a creative imagination.

What Is Creative Imagination?

It is the thing inside of you that machinery can't give you; for it is the ability of your mind to think up ways and means to help others, to ease their aches and complaints, to invent lawnmowers that work easier, potato peelers that save time and can openers that save fingers: things people want and will pay to get.

And the best part of this creative imagination inside us all is that age doesn't have any bearing on its presence.

Somerset Maugham put it this way (and he is over 80 years of age): "Imagination grows by exercise. Contrary to common belief, it is more powerful in the mature than in the young."

Osburn points out that Churchill ran a government on sound imagination of what to say and do to other governments to keep them in line. Grandma Moses, of course, is a classic example of a woman using imagination late in life and becoming world famous as a painter.

Ben Franklin turned out his best work in "old age."

Thomas Jefferson had his best ideas after 80.

Your Most Important Quality

Dr. Albert Einstein said: "Imagination is more important than knowledge," and he set out to prove it himself.

Look around you at successful people without diplomas!

Henry Ford, who left school at about the 6th grade, made a car and changed the entire living scheme of Americans. Edison, who lasted only until the 4th grade—and others around you smoking big cigars, driving big cars (or expensive foreign ones), living high on the hill-top overlooking the city—all men and women without formal education—but certainly not lacking in nature's gift to us all: *imagination*.

Women Also Have This Quality

Osburn's studies proved women have great imagination, which is why they have invented (or prodded others to invent) a pot handle that won't burn fingers; ice cubes that pop out; mops that sop up water quickly.

All products of the feminine imagination.

And what is more, these women are not engineers—have no education in science or manufacturing.

H. W. Hoover, of that famous vacuum cleaner firm, once explained to me why he asked his men to ask women, "What do you want in a vacuum cleaner?" They told the men, who reported back to the firm, and the engineers did the rest of the job.

That is why Hoover put a headlight on his machine, for women said, "I can't see dirt in dark corners."

They put a red signal-light on the Hoover because women would use it long after the bag was loaded, and complained they couldn't tell when the bag was filled. The salesmen then told women prospects, "You may forget to clean the Hoover, but the Hoover won't forget to remind you."

A Mayor Solves an Idea

The imagination of Mayor Earle Cabell, of Dallas, led him to see that stores needed an automatic way of delivering the new trading stamps being issued with merchandise. He hired Charlie Stansell to perfect a stamp machine that the store clerk dials, just as one dials his phone, and the proper amount of stamps come out.

Thus the big complaint of store managers ("It takes time to give stamps"), was solved once and for good.

Imagination—that's what gets you places in life, and you don't have to be a mechanical wizard to think up these simple ideas helpful today in easing work for others.

Imagination is Often Off-Reservation

"Fine," you say, "that is all right for people in a business. They can see what is needed, then hire proper mechanics to perfect some device. That is not possible for me." But that is not always so.

Osburn points out Robert Fulton, for example, an artist who invented the steamboat.

Eli Whitney, a school teacher, invented the cotton gin.

And Samuel Morse, a sculptor and designer, who came up with the telegraph system.

Often you get a better, distant view point, by not being actively in the business. You can see the trees despite the forest.

So let your imagination run wild—without reservation. The wilder the better.

The Suggestion Boxes in Life

In every factory today is the Suggestion Box.

As someone once said, "In every employee is a hidden idea. Let's get it out of them."

And it works.

For the Suggestion Box (itself a product of someone's imagination) now tops the imaginations of workers.

As you go through your daily chores, see what you can put into your own kitchen Suggestion Box. Write little notes to yourself. "I need a broom that won't scatter dust."—"I need a can opener that doesn't cut my fingers."—"I need corks that don't crumble when I pull them from bottles."—"I need caps on medicine bottles that a child can't open."

I need. I need. I need.

Ask yourself what you need—what others may need—then see what you can do to produce the answer.

That's how to go places in life financially—by helping others.

It Can Be Fun, Too

If you keep your eyes open, you will see many things that people need.

I like the one Osburn points out about a man with a lively and creative imagination who noted that baby pigs were often crushed by their mother rolling over them. So he asked whether this couldn't be stopped by simply tilting the floor in the furrowing house.

Sure enough: it worked.

The Department of Agriculture says that these tilted floors have cut pig mortality 25%.

Another farmer saw if he placed his turkey houses on the side of a hill the dung would roll away, and not get messed up in the turkeys.

How simple can you get?

People have found easy ways of making wash and dry clothing; eliminated having to starch shirt collars; made ties that clasp the collar without tying; and seen a thousand other needs for which people will pay.

So keep your eyes open!

That's how soda straws were invented; how scotch tape was invented; how elastic shoe laces for fat boys who couldn't bend over to tie their shoes came to be; and how the wheel barrow, itself, was invented.

All by people who had their eyes open, and saw the need.

How to Get Started

To get started—START.

That's the simplest advice I know.

Make it a point right now to carry a pad and pencil with you, and when you see a conductor fumble for money to make change, ask yourself: "What better way could he do it?"

When you see a mechanic under a car trying to locate leaky oil, ask yourself, "What other way might he do it?"

One mechanic asked that question, and invented a mirror like the dentist uses to see cavities in your teeth (itself an imaginative invention), and today in many garages you'll see mechanics with elongated mirrors peering around engines without getting under them.

And all made money.

Look for Improvements

A wife says, "The can opener is okay for right handed people, but how about us south paws?"

That gave someone an idea for a left-handed can opener.

A man got disgusted raking leaves, so invented a device to put on his lawnmower to mulch them. Now we have the Leaf Mulcher on the market to make husbands happy—and to make money for the imaginative inventor.

Look for improvements. You don't need to invent a brand new item, but just an improvement.

The Story of Harry Ernstrom

Harry saw blind people asking to have needles threaded for them. He saw women using bifocals to thread needles. He figured there must be a simpler way, and he found it.

He found a simple device being sold in Germany.

Harry didn't invent it. But he saw a market for the gadget, and brought it to America, where today thousands of the blind merely lay a thread across a simple one-dollar device, and with one push automatically thread the needle.

So even if you don't invent objects—invent ways of using things already invented.

Find people who can use such items, and it is as good as inventing the device to start with.

New Uses for the Old

Someone invented nylon thread.

Then others invented new uses for nylon, so today you find it even in thread, as well as in stockings—thread to sew garments so the garment will last under abnormal conditions of use.

Someone invented steel. Others invented new uses of it, so that today you sleep on steel! Not horse hair.

And so it goes: some invent objects, others invent new uses. A chap had trouble keeping his flash light in place repairing mechanical devices, so fastened a magnet to the light to hold it in place wherever he worked. Now it is on the market.

You don't need to be a chemist or a mechanical engineer to find things people want, and will pay money to get.

No sooner was hi-fi on the market when someone invented stereo. Then someone else came along with a four track stereo tape recorder, so you can get double the use of the tape —and save money.

What's next?

Maybe you have the answer. Maybe someone else. But why not you?

The World Is Always Changing

Just a few years ago we went to the movies, or stayed home nights to listen to radio. Today it is television that absorbs our attention, the brain child of Dr. DuMont.

We used to swat flies and mosquitos with fly swatters—

today we have aerosol bombs. Once we got up with a dollar alarm clock we had to wind daily; now we get up to radio music. Once we flew with propellors, now we fly with jet propulsion.

Look how our shaving process has changed. And our clothing going from buttons to zippers.

As A. Larkin, Jr., vice-president of Maxwell House, puts it, "It's change that keeps the world moving."

He tells how we used to grind coffee beans. Then they came pre-ground for us. Now instant coffee, such as his Yuban, is on the market. So are television dinners and pre-packaged foods of all sorts that don't require any kitchen work except heating.

All the brain children of imaginative people.

And the end isn't in sight. So look around you for an idea or two to make life easier, more interesting—relieve someone of work, provide more leisure, and you'll find a gold mine yourself.

Gold Mines All Around You

All around you (especially between your ears) are gold mines.

You don't need to go around the world to find them. Dr. Russel Conwell proved this in his famous speech, "Acres of Diamonds," where he cited example after example of men who sold their homes to seek diamonds and oil around the world, only to learn the person who bought his homestead found diamonds and oil right on his own land.

So go into your back yard. Your kitchen. Your work shop. Your place of business. Maybe here is where gold lies for you.

And remember the wisdom of Alex Osburn: there is a gold mine between your ears.

"The essential thing is often not to find—but to absorb what we already know."

People Want To Be Individuals

If you want better workmanship around you, give people a chance to be individual.

In an article in *National Geographic Magazine,* writer Peter T. White tells of a trip to South Viet Nam, where he met Kurt Hinterkopf, a German setting up a toothpaste tube factory.

"I never saw such individualists," said Kurt. "I showed a man exactly where I wanted the faucets. When I came back the faucets were set much higher.

"I asked the man why? 'Look,' he said to me, 'if I am going to work for you, you must let me make some decisions myself.' "

Mixon has a cute answer for this. He quotes a Russian proverb: "If only one evil woman lived on earth, every man would claim she was his wife."

Tip: *Don't underestimate those around you. They may be the boss the next time you see them!*

When you deal with overly shrewd business men, remember another motto: "No melon peddler cries bitter melons . . . no wine dealer sells sour wine."

This, too, is a Russian motto. And if our State Department knew of this ancient Russian proverb, they'd perhaps weigh even more carefully everything said by a modern Russian salesman!

Another Good Philosophy

One good philosophy in life is to let people become part of your act.

"I got many others to help me," says Mixon. "I couldn't do it all myself, but I was always quick to bring people into my act. I invited bankers and realtors, chain store owners and those running big department stores, *to join with me*—I made them part of my suburban daydreams, and they responded because they were part of the show."

Whenever you can get people into the act, do so.

They'll take greater interest.

It is a strategy to use in the home, too. Make the family part of the act of running the home. Let each have his part. He will respond better, and help you build the Castle.

People like to be part of the big show.

That's a tactic to use in fund raising. Give all an assignment. Make them part of the project, not just a "worker."

And one last big trick is: Don't criticize—but praise!

Surely something they are doing merits praise. Find it.

Highlight it. And that person will soon strengthen his weak point, and become your best "cheer leader."

After listening to George Mixon's success in Dallas, I'm glad I lent him a dollar bill.

I'm part of Mixon's success—well, one dollar's worth.

"Change clothes you can; you cannot change the man."

Two Malicious Words

They are, "They say!"
Whenever anyone gets you aside and says, "They say—" be prepared to hear a malicious rumor.
For these are the world's two most malicious words.
Avoid them!
And make yourself a friendly friend.

29

To get along in life
you must learn these ways
to get along with each other
on the job

"The business of life is to go forward."

The quickest way I know to "get along" on the job is to learn to "get along" with the people you work with.

Over 90% of workers fail on their assigned jobs not because of lack of knowledge or skill, but because they can't seem to "fit in" or otherwise "get along" with one another.

Your First Step

The first step in getting along with people you live with, or work with, is to start the day off on the right foot. Not the left. The *right*.

This means a cheerful "Good morning," given with a genuine smile, and not a grunt. Then it acts as a tonic to pep up others, it's a "friend-maker." A tested way to set the stage for the day's performance.

It is corny—but so are all famous success proverbs—to tell you to get up smiling, yet it is the smile that does most in setting the day's pace.

Try your smile on for size in the bathroom.

Before you present it to others, give it the once over.

Then smile at the first people you see. Keep right on smiling throughout the day—from conductor to waitress, to boss to customer to casual acquaintance back to conductor.

Smiles are contagious.

Thus you might say Step One is:

Get Out of Bed on the Right Side!

Then Keep the Ball Rolling

If you start your day off with frowns and grunts and complaints (being a sore head), others around you will reflect you as does the mirror, and your day will be spoiled.

So start the day off with a song in your heart.

Then keep the song humming throughout the day; for the person who is only cheerful until the orange juice wears off at 10:00 a.m. hasn't much ability to get along with others after that time.

Once you've learned to pitch the day in the right KEY, the right tone of harmony and good cheer, then keep it at that musical pitch all day long.

You spend about one-third of your day with fellow workers. That is a big part of your life—so make the most of it. Even if you feel grumpy and out of sorts, don't let others know.

Laugh, clown—LAUGH!

Give and You Get

You are only happy on the job if other people around you are happy.

So make them happy.

For in so doing, they'll turn around and scratch your back. Well, most of them, but of course not the perpetual grouches.

So let's say this is Step Two to get along on the job: *"Give and you get!"*

When somebody drops her cigarette holder, purse, or whatnot, don't shout, "Clumsy ox." Instead, pick it up.

You may be the next clumsy ox.

Hand a fellow worker a pencil, a tool, something he is looking for that you see first.

Then sit back and watch that person try to do you a favor.

Indeed, it is a selfish way to be happy with others.

Joe Brosnan, of the Grace Lines, tells me how a homely handy man working in the Intercontinental Hotels where Joe once supervised publicity, made life more pleasant for himself by this "give and get" technique.

The handy man was indeed homely. As a child people always poked fun of him, and he almost developed a complex.

But he overcame it by one trait of human relations.

Brosnan told me how the second day on the job the man had an extra piece of apple pie in his lunch box. He offered it to a fellow hotel worker.

The next day it was a pear, a chocolate bar—always something to offer somebody working along side him.

It was nothing big and important like passing out dollar bills—just little things like a candy bar. But soon others began to return his gestures of friendliness. They brought him a home made sandwich such as only their mother could put together. They invited him to nightly affairs.

Soon they forgot how homely the man was, much as they forgot it about Abe Lincoln, because the man set out on the job to "get along" and he did it by doing favors for others.

"Give and ye shall receive."

The Perfect Person

As I've often mentioned in this book, a fast way to lose friends is to be the "perfect person." The Tin God.

We loved to trip up the kid in the fancy Sunday suit, because he strutted by the corner drug store showing off his new suit or his pretty date.

We laughed heartily as a kid when a rich old man or dowager in the movies got socked with a custard pie. It elevated our ego. It made us feel good.

Now maybe it is wrong—but it is certainly human to hate perfection in the people around us—those who are really more skilled and talented than ourselves and never let us forget it. They are the people we "lay for," hoping somewhere along the line to trip them up for a laugh.

It is better to be humble and recognize other's abilities, for they in turn will recognize ours.

Making the Day Shorter

There is one good way to shorten the day to make it run faster from morning till whistle time.

It isn't by arriving fifteen minutes later, or quitting fifteen minutes earlier, sneaking past the boss. Nor is it by stretching the luncheon hour five minutes. These only add to the length of the day for then you become "clock conscious." You think too much about the time, and like a watched pot that never boils, the hands of a watched clock never move.

The smart worker has better ways to shorten working hours, and take the drag and monotony out of his work: he does this by making his working life as much a pleasure and fun as a vacation.

I'm not jesting. *It can be done.*

To be sure, it is a trick, but it works magically.

We go, for example, to a party at seven o'clock and stay till midnight, nearly a day's work. But because we are having fun the time passes quickly.

That, then, is the trick: *make work fun, and the day is shortened.*

*

Look around you for pleasures on the job. Some assignments are rough, but others can be made fun, if you have fun in mind; learn the tricks of taking the sting out of the assignment and leaving in the pleasures.

How to Get a Promotion

Want a promotion? Need more money?

It isn't too difficult for the smart person, for it is done by one rule: *always be underpaid!*

At first this sounds ridiculous. But it isn't.

It is far better to be worth more than you are paid, than to be paid more than you are worth.

If you want to ride through depressions in life and not be fired, be the person who always earns more than his pay envelope shows. Then your job is secure. The boss hates to let you go.

It sounds illogical, but the underpaid make the most money!

The Man from Sears

Charlie Kelstadt is now chairman of the board of Sears Roebuck.

I knew him as a store manager in the Cleveland store, then area manager in a Southern district—now he is head of the firm.

Kelstadt got his first promotion, he told me, by being underpaid. Yet never once did he say, "They pay me only for what I do, so why overdo it?"

He attracted attention by doing more work than he was required, until one day a boss said, "Charlie, I can't raise your salary any more on your present job, but I have another job in another city that pays more. Will you take it?"

Sure Charlie took it.

Then he started all over again to be underpaid.

He kept up this tactic until he became president of Sears.

I am sure he is making certain he is still underpaid.

The Cause and the Cure

When a machine goes wrong, the foreman and his mechanics try to find the cause so they can cure the trouble. They don't take a sledge hammer and beat up the machinery in anger.

The same is true in dealing with human nature. When somebody next to you is in trouble, don't be first to yell, "Listen, sour puss, cut the beefing. It annoys me." Instead, find the cause of the other's trouble.

Maybe his wife is sick that day and a kind word from you will make him feel happier and help solve his troubles and stop his beefing. It will help him—and relieve you of the beefing that is annoying to your nerves.

No one can afford to hold a grudge—for it is the most expensive thing you can own. It is almost sure to cost you a raise or a promotion—maybe even your job, which is too much to pay to hold a grudge.

So if you have eyes on getting ahead, recognize the grudges of others—and in yourself—and overcome them. For they are stumbling blocks in life's progress down the Road to Success.

How to Advance on the Job

You can't raise yourself by putting your feet on other people's shoulders to shove yourself up, as you push them down.

That's a trick all leaders soon learn, often the hard way.

Being a "tattle tale" won't get you places either.

When somebody makes a mistake and you run to the boss with the information, you haven't progressed. Even the boss doesn't like you—and certainly the one who made the mistake doesn't like you. Everybody calls you a "snitcher."

When Mom says to a child, "I'll tell your Dad about this," the child is resentful. And Dad isn't too happy either. The teacher who threatens to tell the parents about a child's errors doesn't cure the errors.

It is better to flow easily through life than to set up stumbling blocks. You'll earn a friend, a promotion, a salary increase, by learning the ways to make others happy. In return they'll respond and make you happy.

Three Tested Rules to Hold a Job

1. *Stop HOLDING BACK on the Job.*

   "Holding back" on the job uses up as much energy as doing twice the work. "Doing nothing," say work psychologists, "tires us more than a hard day's work."
   How often have you said, "Gosh, doing nothing all day tires me out more than if I'd been at my regular job."

2. *Make Your Work a "Game."*

   There is one big difference between work and play, and it is this: play is something we do because we enjoy doing it, while work is something we MUST do.
   Thus work tires us out, and play rests us.
   It's the same trick again of making a game out of the job.

Tom Sawyer did it in white-washing a fence, to a point that his boy friends actually paid him for the privilege of doing the white-washing!

3. *Become a "Star" Performer.*

It is a psychological fact that we like to do anything that we do unusually well.

"Star performers" in the circus, on stage, in the movies, on TV get a big kick, a thrill, out of their work, and thus they become star attractions.

Dr. Ernest Dichter's survey of housewives showed that the women who were really good cooks were the ones who "simply loved to cook."

We love to do what others believe we excel in doing.

Kinds of Workers in Life

Know people and what makes them "tick," and you'll get along better with them and shorten the working hours, and go places in life.

Here are some typical types of fellow workers. Any you know?

THE FRIEND MAKER

She makes friends easily. Customers walk for extra blocks just to get her advice and give her their business. She has a pleasant smile, twinkling eyes, understanding and sympathy. A good type for you to imitate.

THE LEADER

He makes fast decisions. He is on his toes. He understands people. He worked himself to the top of his department. He will understand your problems. Place confidence in him—mimic his ability!

THE DETAILER

He likes details. He can find pins in a haystack or add a column of figures that would bewilder and confuse you. But he keeps things running, so appreciate this quality in him. He is the "heart" that runs the store or plant.

THE BULLY

Avoid him. He is a "tough guy." He bullies you because he is "out" to cover up his weak points and failings. He has an inferiority complex. He tries to "hide it" behind a loud mouth. He'll soon tone down or move on, so side step him.

THE SULKER

She is "too good for the job." She thinks she should be a big shot executive right off the bat. She sulks on the job, shirks her work, passes the buck. She won't last long so don't bother with her.

THE HONEST WORKER

This is the "understanding type." A good sport. He is honest with you and with his job. The salt of the earth. Try to be this person yourself.

There are of course many other types of fellow workers—the clown, the jokester, the gossip; the factory griper and the office shirker; the flirt and the lazy person.

But try to be the NORMAL TYPE. They form the background of the everyday world; not the great genius or inventor, but the person who keeps the wheels moving smoothly in industry and the business world.

The Story of Samuel Vauclain

Sam Vauclain had about as monotonous a job as you could imagine. He worked on a lathe turning out bolts. The same thing over and over, day after day. Then one day he made "the grind a game."

Turning to a fellow worker he said, "Let's see who can turn out the most bolts. You rough them off on your machine and I'll finish them on mine. We'll see who can do it faster. If we get tired we can swap jobs."

The two "star" performers began to enjoy the job, for it became a game of skill, good workmanship and pride . . . and the days became shorter.

Who is Samuel Vauclain?

Well, dear reader, the chap ended up the "game" by becoming just the president of the Baldwin Locomotive Works.

His success secret?

This: "Get a kick out of your job."

SELF-CONFIDENCE AND SUCCESS

(As observed by A. H. Kulikowsky, Publisher, *Salesman's Opportunity Magazine*)

This summer I walked into the office of a leading sales executive, a man who operates a multi-million dollar company. It was a handsome office and I complimented him on the furnishings and the expensive pictures that covered the walls.

I was curious, however, about a large, cheaply framed motto that hung in the center of the wall above his desk. It simply said . . . SMILE. Before I left my curiosity got the best of me and I asked whether there was a special reason for giving it the place of honor in his office.

"When I began this business almost thirty years ago," he told me, "I would often work sixteen and eighteen hours a day. I had a little office in a loft that was stifling in summer and freezing in winter. My wife often had to patch the only pair of pants I owned and there were many times when her tiny salary as a clerk in a department store paid the rent for our little apartment and bought our groceries.

"One day I came home, after a long and disappointing day, and told her that it was no use. I had failed.

"She pleaded with me to give it six months more . . . she asked only that I look on the bright side. Yes, it was uphill all the way. It was rough. But, if it worked out, and it might, our sacrifices would be repaid.

"A few days later she slipped into my office and hung that motto over my desk. It forced me to smile . . . to laugh . . . to forget my troubles for the moment. Every time I had to deal with someone who was getting my goat, I'd look at it . . . and my sense of humor would return. If I was disappointed, I felt obliged to see the silver lining. It made a big difference in me and my sales.

"Over the years, I've gotten a reputation for being a man who is self-confident, pleasant and easy to do business with. This reputation, I feel, is the backbone of my business. I've learned that self-confidence and success are inseparable in selling.

"Although I feel that I no longer need to be told to 'smile,' since it has become a second nature, I never want to forget the importance of being contented, confident and pleasant. Don't you think that it deserves the place of honor in my office?"

I certainly did! I also felt that he had an important message for everyone. If you can master the secret of inner contentment if you can retain your serenity in the face of difficult problems . . . if you can overcome discouragement you will have the ingredients of the self-confidence you need to succeed.

All of us have much to be thankful for. We have many blessings on the credit side of the ledger of life. At this, the Thanksgiving season, it's especially appropriate for us to review them.

Remember your blessings. Make it a practice to *smile*. Concentrate on the positive side of your life and your work. Doing these things will give you a confident personality. It will make you the kind of person people trust, admire and respect. Above all, it will make you a successful salesman!

30

Six steps to get ahead faster in life

"You will never be a leader unless you first learn to follow."—Tiorio

Way 1:

Admit it when you are wrong.
In so doing you help the other person "be right," and that is a mighty good tactic in making friends and avoiding enemies. Be quick to say, "I must be in error." Be fast to observe, "I believe I did this wrong."
In so doing, you help the other fellow be right.
And that goes a long way in maintaining leadership among mankind.

Way 2:

"I am counting on you!"
If you want to make people feel good, and get the best from them, try these five magic words, "I am counting on you."

Way 3:

Give people an incentive.
Offer them "little white bribes." Candy for the children; the

car for the son; a meal downtown for Mom—and something for poor old Dad.

Give the workers around you an incentive to work better—to like you better, if it is only an occasional cup of coffee, cigar, a good time on the town.

Even the donkey walks faster when a carrot is hung before his eyes.

Way 4:

Leave 'em with a good taste.

President Kennedy leaves 'em with a smile on his face, despite the tension of the moment. General MacArthur said, "I shall return." He did.

If you can't make the sale then and there, at least leave 'em with a friendly feeling. Never with a blunt "NO" on their tongue. Always with a "perhaps," "maybe," "some other day."

Leave 'em with a friendly taste of your visit, whether business or social.

Way 5:

Don't correct others—help them!

Be alert to point out errors, but only in a helpful manner. Never shout, "You did it wrong!" Instead, try this medicine: "Here, let me help you!" Or, "I used to do it that way, but let me show you a way that someone taught me that is better."

This is a wonderful way to maintain friends, and get things done the way you want.

Way 6:

Relax the other person.

Before any sale is made of anything, from a product to a friendship, the other person must first be relaxed.

Some sellers relax the customer with a good luncheon; others tell an amusing story; others find some hobby, or object in the prospects room, to discuss before the business.

Smiling relaxes others. Sitting relaxed—relaxes others. Laughter will relax.

Subhana the Worst, famed seller in Kashmir, India, relaxed me (and others) in his showroom by saying, "I am not in the mood today to sell, only to show."

A relaxed dog is easier to teach tricks.

Learn the Tactful Ways

If you will put these six steps to work for you, the day won't be far when you are a leader among people.

Lee was quick to admit he, not Pickett, was wrong, when he said, "I and I alone have lost this battle."

Lord Chesterfield said: "Be wiser than other people, if you can, but do not tell them."

Lincoln often remarked, "A drop of honey catches more flies than a gallon of gall," and he won people to his way of thinking by watching his words.

You, too, can lead men . . . win over others . . . by such principles.

Good lawyers always use tact with such phrases as, "Gentlemen, do not overlook these facts."—"May I call this to your attention."—"With your understanding of people, I know you will agree. . . ."

This is a tactful way of showing the jury the facts without insulting their intelligence, of inviting their vote without a sledge hammer in your hand.

"The bow that's always bent will quickly break;
But if unstrung will serve at your need."
—Phaedrus

An Anecdote About Selfishness

It is interesting to note, from such men as the Most Reverend Fulton J. Sheen, that the words *selfish* and *selfishness* were unknown until about 300 years ago.

To be sure selfishness is as old as sin. It has always been a sin to think only of yourself, but only in recent times has selfishness —the love of one's self—become noted by psychologists and teachers as a deterrent to self-progress.

Selfish people burn up needless energy, getting nowhere fast.

When a person is obviously looking out for the "great number one, I," you are as cautious of him as when you are told to beware of snakes in the pasture. It is the big hearted person in disguise that we must beware of, as brought out in this story I love to tell:

It is about a selfish architect in Egypt. On a tower he carved his name in the rock, but covered it with plaster. Then upon the plaster he put the King's name in gold leaf. Naturally the King was highly flattered by this altruistic architect, until time soon crumbled the plaster, the gold leaf with the name of the King washed off—and the architect's name stared down upon the world.

*

You will never properly relax caring only for yourself, warns Bishop Sheen. Your own self is too small a prison, he says, in which to relax, caring only for yourself. "For that is like a serpent swallowing his own tail."

Only in being thoughtful of others, can you relax.

Many have heard this story in India, as I did. Told to me by Dr. Brij Myer, it is about a rice grower who learned of irrigation. The first year his irrigation waters overflowed into the field of his neighbor, who also then had a fine crop of rice.

"Why should I do that?" asked the rice grower, and so the next season he built a dam around his field to prevent the irrigated waters from flowing away. The result was the water remained confined but in so doing rotted out his rice. His land had turned to swamp.

*

To overcome selfishness puts you on the right road to personal success. When you help others; when you share your good fortune; when you listen more than you speak, at those moments you go places faster in life. To so give, makes you feel great!

Think you—not I.

Give to receive!

Help others to get along in life, and you'll help yourself get along with others, and go places.

"Light a candle for the Devil, too: *you never know!*"

31

A condensation
of ways to win others
and avoid enemies!

"Desire of greatness is a god-like sin!"

Handling Arguments

Be wrong!

That's the simplest way to handle complaints. Let the other fellow be right—well, at least in the beginning of things. Later on he will be easier to convince.

Give in on details.

That's another trick in disarming an opponent, or an objector of any sort. Agree he is right on certain items. List them. Agree. Then hold out on a major item—or swap a few agreements, of minor nature, for this one big thing you want a "yes" on.

The Russians are experts on this system. They are constantly upsetting the world, starting troubles—little troubles. They are then willing to give in on the smaller ones to gain a minor objective.

They will blind our eyes with "little wars." Then dare us with a big one. We rush in. They agree on details—but they always hold out for the big issues, like Hungary or Berlin. Watch their technique. It is a pattern, always the same.

They act—we react!

Giving Criticisms

One last thought on the technique of telling people how to do a better job. The trick being: be *amusing, humorous,* or otherwise give the criticism with lightness of spirit.

A sudden roar of disapproval, and you'll ruin goodwill.

The other day at a friend's home I observed tact in handling a helper. This helper had a bad habit of standing the broom with the bristles down, and this of course soon bends the bristles. No amount of preaching did any good in reminding the helper not to do this. Then one day the lady of the house took over. She said:

"You'll have bad luck all day long if you place the broom with the bristles down—besides the broom won't clean as good."

At once the helper took interest. He wanted good luck. He wanted the work to go easier and faster. From then on, he never stood the broom with the bristles down.

That's what I mean about there being an art to criticism.

*

William G. McAdoo, under Woodrow Wilson, once said, "You can't defeat an ignorant man by argument!"

It takes tact!

Losing at Games

Many a salesman golfer plays what is called "customer's golf." That's letting the customer win for business reasons, the reasons being he is apt to give more business to people *he* can whip at golf.

I think a classic example of letting the other person win was used by Constant, the head valet in Napoleon's household. He always let Josephine win at billiards, saying, "Although I had some skill, I always managed to let her beat me, which pleased her exceedingly." And, naturally, Josephine employed the same tactics with old Nap. You'll get farther in life, home or outside, by letting other people have the thrill of winning. It will give you more kick to see them happy this way, than to win yourself. Your happiness can create envy in the other person, and soon you'll be unhappy yourself. Try the art of letting others win at bridge or golf— and you will be inwardly more happy watching your skill in handling people to win them over, than to win them over in the game itself.

*

The best way to get the better of any argument with others is to avoid it in the first place.

*

You will avoid making enemies by letting others be right. Any wife knows this by heart. Hubby is always right—well, to himself, anyway, and that's mighty good wifely tact.

If necessary, put words in the mouths of others by saying, "I like the way you want this plan carried out."

It was your plan; but you were too wise to let the other person know. So you agreed on "his plan." Wives do this instinctively!

Socrates, the wise one, would disarm an enemy by saying that there was one thing he knew, and that was "I know nothing."

Starting with this disarming premise, Socrates proceeded

to put words into the other person's mouth—Socrates' own words that the other person believed were his own!

*

Never say: *"I'll show you how right I am!"*
Better to say: *"Do you think I am on the right track?"*
Avoid: *"You are 100% wrong!"*
Say: *"I agree with almost everything you say, but what is your opinion of this idea?"*

*

Exercising Self-Control

At times you want to blurt out, "All right—do it your way, but you'll see I'm right!"

Better to say, "Perhaps you are right. Why not go ahead with your plan." Often the other person then becomes frightened of his own idea, and may say, "Well, maybe so—maybe not. I'm not too sure now."

Exercise self-control at such moments. Never be fast to blurt out an objection. Rather feed it *into* the discussion tactfully. Bring up your idea in a matter-of-fact way, saying, "Your ideas are all fine. I once thought of another way to do it. What do you think?" Then tell your plan. It weaves itself delicately into the discussion. It then has a chance to take seed.

It is often tactful to let an imaginary third person speak for you, saying, "My attorney once tried a similar case this way, and found it worked. How do you like his plan?"

It isn't your idea. It is someone outside the discussion circle.

Often you can pick out a famous person on whom to tag your idea. Someone who has had more experience than any-

one present. Often you can quote a famous proverb to prove
the point. All of which lets you out. It is not your plan, so
no one present will get envious and be jealous of your proposal.

The Tact of Ferris Mack

Ferris Mack, successful senior editor of Doubleday, has a
tactful method in handling disgruntled authors who write
him how wrong he is. Mack holds his tongue. He exercises
self-control. He will write them: "Come to think about it a
second time, maybe you are right. Next time you are in town
drop in and see me."

In most cases, the upset author forgets the matter. He
rested his complaint on Mack's willingness to believe him
right!

Always start a discussion by admitting the other person
may be right!

Don't Remake Others

Husbands and wives try to make each other over, and that
is a sure way to head to the divorce courts. It is better to
learn to live with another person's personality than to try
to change him.

If something must be changed, then be tactful about it.

No one is perfect—and it is wiser to bend with the other,
so that they will bend with you.

At times you can compromise and say, "We all have faults
in our make up that annoy others. Mine are the following.
I'll try to change them. Will you help by trying to change
things that seem to bother me?"

A fair exchange is no robbery!

Be Quick to Appreciate

Leaders in business are quick to show appreciation, an important trait in winning goodwill among workers.

Learn this art of appreciating the other person. Be quick to tell him of your appreciation.

It means much to others, especially wives. Be alert to a new dress, a new hat—a new menu. Appreciate the little lady, and watch how carefully she will watch the budget—and watch your taste buds!

People who can appreciate—are themselves appreciated.

Give a Little Attention

This is an art for both the gentleman and the gentle lady. They pay full attention to those who are talking.

Too often one wants to interrupt someone. Too often one wants to rush off in the middle of a sentence. Don't. Pay a little attention. You'll go places faster with that person if you pay attention.

Be courteous to the other person. Show good manners.

If you want people to pay attention to you when you talk, then pay attention when they talk.

It All Boils Down to This

1. Give in on details.
2. Make criticisms in a light vein.
3. Lose—let others win.
4. Exercise self-control!
5. Don't expect to reform the other person.
6. Be quick to appreciate others.
7. Give your undivided attention.

"Hitch your wagon to a star."

"—the lack of an alternative."

IF YOU ARE LUCKY ENOUGH
TO POSSESS THIS VALUED INGREDIENT
YOUR SUCCESS IS "POSITIVELY GUARANTEED"

- Ask me what the greatest of all success secrets is, and I am apt to give you this ancient formula, *"—the lack of an alternative."*
- Ask me what I think is the world's greatest of all motivators of mankind, and I would again tell you, *"—the lack of an alternative."*
- Ask me then, for the most magical of all ingredients (if there is such a magic) that would give you a "positive guarantee" to success, and again most certainly I will tell you, *"—the lack of an alternative."*

What Is This "Magical Ingredient?"
How Does It Work?

"—the lack of an alternative" means no other way was open to you, so you could only go forward.

You had no place to turn—no where else to go—you had to prod on and go places, or else fall in defeat.

This lack of an alternative pushed you forward.

There was no back-tracking for you, no side roads or detours —just the long, hard road ahead. You were not given an alternative. You had no escape hatch, no emergency exit nor shelter in which to hide.

Therefore you kept going forward!

The Success of Israeli Is Modern Proof

All through history you read of successful people, of successful kingdoms, and on close study you will find that most of these successes were due to a lack of "no where else to go."

But perhaps the most striking example of the potency of this great Law of Success, *the lack of an alternative,* is the modern founding of the Land of Israeli "on sands and stones and rugged shore lines."

Ships arrived daily with displaced people. The ships disgorged them. Where else could they go? Where else could they dig in but on these rugged shores, long since abandoned by people ahead of them? For they lacked an alternative. A promised land. None was offered to them.

So they dug in for self-preservation.

And, well, you know the story from here on. A new land was founded and formed in a single decade by displaced people with no other place to go, no alternative.

So be lucky if you suddenly find you are at an impasse in life —with no place to turn. In so lacking an alternative, you will be *forced* down the road to Success.

Fortunate is the person who lacks an alternative!

WARNING!

Success Can Make Failures of People
Failures Can Make Successes of People

Recently I had the pleasure of hearing Rabbi Levi Olan speak on "The Lonely Life" at Temple Emanuel in Dallas, Texas. He is a professor of Religion at Southern Methodist University.

Rabbi Olan pointed out to an audience of many creeds which had gathered to hear him, that successful people often develop an inferiority complex from their own success, fearing others may take advantage of their success and become friendly only because of the fame they have acquired.

He also pointed out how difficult it is for certain people to "live with" the success of their friends and neighbors, that where people boost their own ego by helping friends in their failures, it is extremely hard for some to accept the successes of others without becoming unjustly jealous and envious.

Rabbi Olan pointed out that often successful people cannot accept their own success, for they live in fear of others; this often drives them to failure again.

In becoming a failure, once more, they feel a load has been taken off them, and they can again feel that they have true friends.

In concluding this book on "how to put yourself across," remember to keep a weather-eye out for the affect your success can have on you, and others around you.

Through caution, you can anticipate Rabbi Olan's warning.

You can guide your success with the same care you used masterfully in obtaining success.

Don't lose out by becoming a success; make success work for you, by the proper sustaining of the success. By the proper handling of yourself your success won't injure others' opinions of you through your attitude.

No one likes the *nouveau riche!*

No one likes the new successes!

So while enjoying success retain your modesty. Don't flaunt it. Don't brag about it. Handle with care. It's fragile.

Be humble. Be yourself.

Don't let success be the cause of your failure!

Meet the Author

Elmer Wheeler is a former newspaperman who created the business formula, "Don't Sell the Steak—Sell the Sizzle."

He took this wise-crack and built it into an imposing business philosophy, with a string of successes to prove it. Over 247 firms around the world now use The Sizzler's friend-making and business-getting ideas.

Some years ago we asked Elmer to write a book on how to sell yourself to others. He did just that and so named his book, *How To Sell Yourself To Others.*

Over the years it has become a tremendous success and has been translated into innumerable foreign languages, for all the world seemed interested in Sizzler Elmer's ideas of how to get along with people, plus the many strategies and techniques he has invented or collected to help people go places.

Famous Fat Boy Author

Elmer is also the author of *The Fat Boy's Book,* that received acclaim in *Time, Newsweek, The New Yorker* and other magazines. For Elmer came up with amusing, practical, and highly valuable tips on how to slice off the "fat of the land."

He has been written up twice in *Reader's Digest* and *Fortune,* and was discussed most favorably on a Mike Wallace interview TV program.

He is author of such books as, *Tested Selling Tips From Around The World; Around The World With Elmer, Backwards; The Wealth Within You;* and his classic books, *How To Make Your Sales Sizzle in 17 Days; Tested Sentences That Sell;* and his latest big seller, *Selling Dangerously.* He has written 23 books in all.

A Popular Speaker and Writer

Once *American Business Magazine* asked 500 groups who their most popular speaker had been in the "how to" field, and Elmer won hands down with 125% more votes than the runner-up.

His talk, "How To Get Along With Others," has been given more than 6,000 times, more frequently than any other talk including the famous "Acre of Diamonds" talk by Dr. Russell Conwell.

His popularity has attracted television producers. He has appeared with Groucho Marx, Art Linkletter, Jack Paar and such programs as To Tell the Truth—for Elmer is most down to earth in his newsy, breezy newspaper style of speaking and writing.

His Newest and Best Yet

This is Elmer's newest book. It is his best yet. It will bring you up to date on all the methods, techniques and strategy used, not only in America to win friends, but from around the world.

He constantly brings out methods used worldwide to make friends. He has discovered many ways to get along in life as used for centuries by people of other lands, but never practiced in the United States. He will tell you, for example, about the soft sell of Japan; the bargain ways of Hong Kong;

the winning silk appeals of Bangkok people; the image sell of India and so forth—how these people sell themselves to others and go places in life.

Truly, this is a collection of best ways—and test ways—to make friends, keep old friends—and go places.

You'll live, you'll learn, you'll become a master of self-sell, once you've read these lively chapters of Mr. Sizzle.

THE PUBLISHER